White River Junction and the Connecticut River, looking south to Mt. Ascutney, 1889. Courtesy Montshire Museum of Scie

THE UPPER VALLEY

An Illustrated Tour Along The

CONNECTICUT RIVER

Before The Twentieth Century

by JEROLD WIKOFF

CHELSEA GREEN PUBLISHING COMPANY, CHELSEA, VERMONT 05038

Library of Congress Cataloging in Publication Data

Wikoff, Jerold, 1945-
     The upper valley.

     Bibliography: p.
     Includes index.
     1. Connecticut River Valley--History.   2. Connecticut
River Valley--Social life and customs.
I. Title.
F12.C7W64   1985   974.2   85-4706

ISBN 0-930031-01-6

for Charlotte,
Alyssa
and Alexander

ACKNOWLEDGEMENTS

CURIOSITY inspired this book. When in 1975 I moved from California to the Upper Valley, I barely knew its location on the map. Nothing of its history was known to me, but I soon became interested. Stone walls running through the woods intrigued me immediately. Why were they there, where it seemed no one could ever have lived? When I chanced across some cellar holes in the middle of the woods, I was hooked. I wanted to know more about the early life in the Upper Valley, when farms rather than trees had obviously covered the rugged hillsides.

Curiosity was the impetus, but an outsider does not know what paths will lead him to the facts. People are needed to guide the way, and a great many have led me. Without their help this book could never have been written.

The *Valley News* came first. In the spring of 1980 preparations were being made to tear down a tannery in the middle of Lebanon. Wanting to know something about the life of those buildings before they disappeared, I proposed writing an article about them. With the help of Russell Powell, features editor at the time, that one article turned into five. And then I was asked to write a weekly column, giving me an excellent reason to explore Upper Valley history. Very quickly the column became a regular part of the newspaper, appearing every Tuesday for almost two years. I thank everyone at the *Valley News* for the lengthy space extended me, for the excellent layout provided weekly, and for the many suggestions given. In particular I thank Bill McCartha, managing editor, for his constant support.

A weekly column means a weekly deadline. To meet it, regularly available sources need to be found. Without the help of Kenneth Cramer and the other librarians in the Special Collections of Baker Library at Dartmouth College, I would have soon faltered. Their resources and help were invaluable. Often a suggestion of Kenneth Cramer's became the idea for next week's column, and numerous times it was pictures from Special Collections which accompanied the articles. I thank also the many other librarians at the Dartmouth College Libraries for their help in finding the books I always wanted in a hurry.

Others also provided valuable assistance in directing me to the right sources. In particular, I would like to thank: Edwin Battison, director of the American Precision Museum in Windsor, who guided me through unfamiliar territory in the development of machine tools; John Berthelsen, curator of maps at Baker Library, who located and drew several helpful maps of the Upper Valley; Cecile Blodgett, who shared her copy of a letter written by Alexander Crummell; Virginia Colby, who gave me invaluable tips about Maxfield Parrish and other matters of Cornish, New Hampshire; Jere Daniell, professor of history at Dartmouth, who provided suggestions and encouragement; John Dryfhout, curator of the Saint-Gaudens National Historic Site, who told me about the history of "Huggins Folly"; Michael Green, professor of native American studies at Dartmouth, who explained much and directed me to almost every book I read about Indians in New Hampshire and Vermont; Alice Doan Hodgson, who continually provided new details about the history of Orford; Robert Leavitt, who gave considerable time and told me about Lebanon's early mills and about Tilden Female Seminary; Edgar Mead, who opened the way to understanding the history of railroads in the

Upper Valley; and John St. Croix, who shared his extensive knowledge of Hartford and White River Junction.

I wish also to thank the many institutions and historical societies which lent assistance whenever asked and which provided the pictures used for my articles and for this book: Alice Peck Day Hospital, the American Precision Museum, the Bailey/Howe Library (Special Collections), Brown & Bigelow, the Claremont Historical Society, Dartmouth College Libraries, the Enfield Historical Society, the Hanover Historical Society, Hirschl & Adler Galleries, the Hood Museum at Dartmouth College, the Lebanon Historical Society, the Lyme Historical Society, Marlboro College, Mary Hitchcock Memorial Hospital, the Montshire Museum of Science, National Life of Vermont, *New England Rail Service*, the New Hampshire Historical Society, the Old Fort No. 4 Associates, the Orford Historical Society, the Pomfret (Vermont) Historical Society, the Rockingham Free Public Library, the Saint-Gaudens National Historic Site, the Vermont Division of Historic Preservation, the Vermont Historical Society, and the Woodstock Historical Society.

To create a book from newspaper articles is a lengthy and detailed process. Without the help of many people I could not have found the thread to weave separate chapters into a unified whole. I thank Charlotte Armster, whose encouragement never faltered; John Rassias, whose enthusiasm convinced me to collect the articles into a book; Frank Janney, who — unknown to me — found a publisher; Ian and Margo Baldwin, whose friendship and continuous editorial advice helped extract the best from me; Jane Curtis, for her attentive comments and enthusiasm; and Frank Lieberman, for innumerable illustrative suggestions. I thank also Mary Pat Brigham, John Dumville, Euclid Farnham, Vernon Field, Daniel Fleetham, Diane Forsberg, Harry Frye, Wendell Hess, Laura Lucky, John Moon, Nancy Muller, John Nevins, Robert Nye, Robert Rhodes, Gwenda Smith, Nadia Smith, Cornelia Swayze, and Walter Wright, many of whom either took time to read chapters, to correct dates and other factual material, or to help locate illustrations. And I thank Susan Edwards for her thoughtful stylistic suggestions and Jeffrey Nintzel for his excellent work in preparing many of the prints for the illustrations.

The list grows long, and still it is not complete. A special thanks goes to the New Hampshire Council for the Humanities, which sponsored numerous lectures in and around the Upper Valley. A great many people attended my lectures and shared with me their experience of New Hampshire's past. Through them I discovered the Upper Valley's history in a personal way not conveyed by books. Many others generously responded to my *Valley News* articles by writing letters with details and suggestions, and some simply stopped me on the street and talked about an article I had written. I wish I could list everyone by name. Hearing from you, meeting many of you was the best part of my learning about the Upper Valley.

ILLUSTRATION SOURCES

THE AMERICAN PRECISION MUSEUM, *Windsor, Vermont.*

BAKER LIBRARY, *Dartmouth College, Hanover, New Hampshire.*

BAILEY/HOWE LIBRARY *(Special Collections), University of Vermont, Burlington, Vermont.*

CHRISTY BARNES, *Hillsdale, New York.*

BROWN & BIGELOW, *St. Paul, Minnesota.*

VIRGINIA COLBY, *Cornish, New Hampshire.*

DANIEL W. FLEETHAM, *Canaan, New Hampshire.*

HIRSCHL & ADLER GALLERIES, INC., *New York City, New York.*

ALICE DOAN HODGSON, *Orford, New Hampshire.*

THE HOOD MUSEUM OF ART, *Dartmouth College, Hanover, New Hampshire.*

LEBANON HISTORICAL SOCIETY, *Lebanon, New Hampshire.*

LYME HISTORICAL SOCIETY, *Lyme, New Hampshire.*

MARY HITCHCOCK MEMORIAL HOSPITAL, *Hanover, New Hampshire.*

MONTSHIRE MUSEUM OF SCIENCE, *Hanover, New Hampshire.*

NATIONAL LIFE OF VERMONT, *Montpelier, Vermont.*

NEW ENGLAND RAIL SERVICE, *c/o Donald B. Valentine, Jr., Newbury, Vermont.*

NEW HAMPSHIRE HISTORICAL SOCIETY, *Concord, New Hampshire.*

PUBLIC ARCHIVES CANADA, *Ottawa, Ontario.*

THE HOWARD RICE COLLECTION, *Marlboro College, Marlboro, Vermont.*

ROCKINGHAM FREE PUBLIC LIBRARY, *Bellows Falls, Vermont.*

SAINT-GAUDENS NATIONAL HISTORIC SITE, *National Park Service, USDI, Cornish, New Hampshire.*

VERMONT DIVISION FOR HISTORIC PRESERVATION, *Montpelier, Vermont.*

VERMONT HISTORICAL SOCIETY, *Montpelier, Vermont.*

WOODSTOCK HISTORICAL SOCIETY, *Woodstock, Vermont.*

Maps by JOHN F. BERTHELSEN, *Chelsea, Vermont.*

TABLE OF CONTENTS

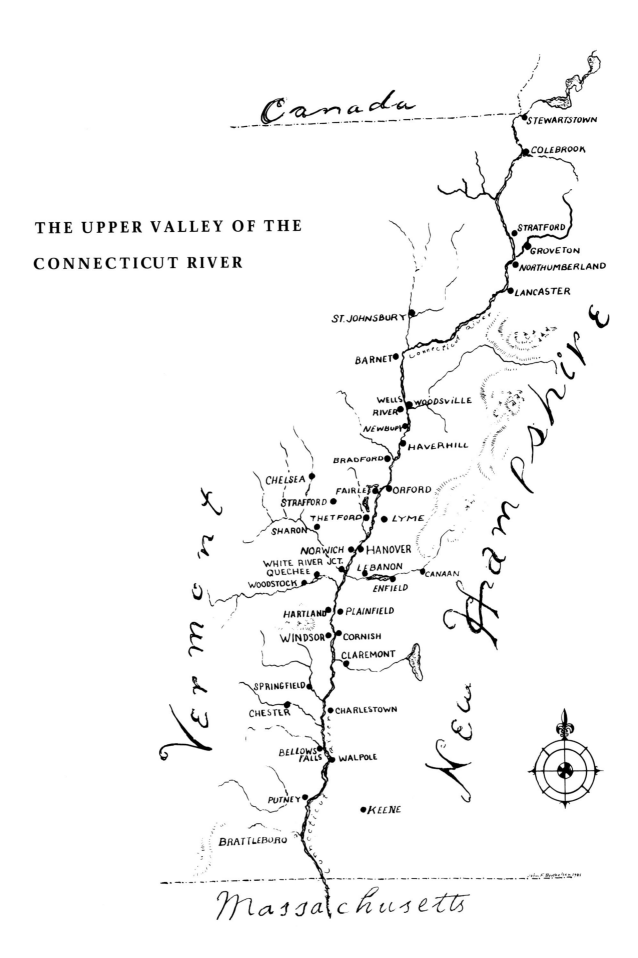

THE UPPER VALLEY OF THE
CONNECTICUT RIVER

Canada

Massachusetts

Vermont

New Hampshire

STEWARTSTOWN
COLEBROOK
STRATFORD
GROVETON
NORTHUMBERLAND
LANCASTER
ST. JOHNSBURY
BARNET
Connecticut River
WELLS RIVER
WOODSVILLE
NEWBURY
HAVERHILL
BRADFORD
CHELSEA
FAIRLEE
ORFORD
STRAFFORD
THETFORD
LYME
SHARON
NORWICH
HANOVER
WHITE RIVER JCT.
QUECHEE
LEBANON
CANAAN
WOODSTOCK
ENFIELD
HARTLAND
PLAINFIELD
WINDSOR
CORNISH
CLAREMONT
SPRINGFIELD
CHESTER
CHARLESTOWN
BELLOWS FALLS
WALPOLE
PUTNEY
KEENE
BRATTLEBORO

John F. Berthelsen 1981

Introduction:

BOUNDARIES OF THE UPPER VALLEY

To BE a New Hampshire native, your grandmother must have been born in the state. And, of course, a mother and father as well. I first heard this definition at a Cornish "Old Home Days" celebration, and since then many others have confirmed its truth. Vermonters, I assume — though I have never been told directly — require a similar passage through three generations to achieve native status.

Having been the first in my family to set foot in either New Hampshire or Vermont — and that in 1975 — I don't even come close. I am just another recent newcomer to the area, and no matter how long I might remain that is what I will always be. That I see myself as a permanent newcomer should not be misconstrued as a personal lament. Nor do I intend any jibe at the ways of those who have have lived in New Hampshire or Vermont for many generations. I am simply accepting the fact that no number of years can ever alter my outsider's perspective. An entire lifetime would never suffice to make me aware of the subtle differences that apparently exist on the two sides of the Connecticut River. In fact, I would probably still continue to think life was exactly the same on either side if a few natives from New Hampshire had not confided to me that Vermonters — even Vermonters right across the water — were, well, somehow different.

These differences simply escape me, and always will. Being a newcomer, I tend to sense similarities rather than differences. Whenever I travel along the northern stretches of the Connecticut, I am struck by the similarity of the towns — on both sides of the river. Seeing a sameness, it seems natural to me that this entire region should commonly be called the Upper Connecticut River Valley. For me, the Upper Valley possesses a cohesion and a unity.

But that is me, the newcomer, speaking. Others do not see it that way, especially others who have the experience of generations. For them, the differences are important, and the term Upper Valley is never used in such a broad sense. To the north, for example, only the upper reaches of the Connecticut River are generally thought of as the Upper Valley. Farther south the term Upper Valley refers rather imprecisely to the middle section of Vermont and New Hampshire, extending southward to Windsor or even Bellows Falls and possibly as far north as Orford. The region even farther south, extending to the Massachusetts border, seems to many to have no regional nomenclature, leaving open the question whether those towns even belong to the Upper Valley.

All this confusion and unclarity about the boundaries of the Upper Valley poses no problems for those living along the river. "The Upper Valley" is simply a convenient and loosely defined term to be used whenever referring to something a bit beyond immediate and local limits. This might mean extending boundaries momentarily to the north or to the south, or maybe even across the river. It does not matter much which. Everyone always understands.

A problem arises, however, when a newcomer arrives who wants to write about the history of the Upper Valley. Boundaries suddenly become important, because now it has to be decided what is to be included in this history, and what left out. If it were simply a choice between newcomer and native, the newcomer would, of course, stand little chance. Who is he, after all, to decide what constitutes the Upper Valley. But the choice is not so simple, for it turns out there are other New Hampshire natives who share a similar unified conception of the Upper Valley. In the southeast, for example, down by Concord and Manchester and on over to Portsmouth, there are a great many who view the entire river stretch as one, cohesive region. This is not always expressed in the most positive

English in the 1630s, the unsettled parts immediately to the north were called "the upper valley." This meant that the river land in Massachusetts was considered the Upper Connecticut Valley. The reference point for the Upper Valley changed as English settlement pushed northward to Deerfield and Northfield, just as the location of the American West shifted after each wave of new settlers.

Eventually almost the entire length of the river above the Massachusetts border was called the Upper Valley. This name became established rather fixedly after nearly a hundred years in which

manner. At its mildest, the river towns are perceived as being "different" from the rest of New Hampshire. On other occasions the entire Upper Valley is referred to as the "Vermont of New Hampshire." This remark is not meant to be an impartial observation about scenic similarities.

That other New Hampshire natives sense a cohesiveness in the river valley, as does the newcomer, is not the only reason to think of the entire stretch of river north from Massachusetts as the Upper Valley. There are historical reasons as well. When the lower reaches of the Connecticut were first occupied by the

northward settlement was halted by a continuous series of wars between the English settlers and the Indians and French. Starting with King Philip's War in 1675 and continuing until the conclusion of the Seven Years War in 1763, the entire stretch of the river north of Northfield, Massachusetts, became a no man's land, open to intermittant raids and battles. Settlement was impossible.

By the 1760s there was a sizeable population in New England, and many people were looking for new land to farm. The end of the Seven Years War resulted in a sudden influx of settlers into most of the northern reaches of the Connecticut River. The entire area was settled at much the same time, and most towns along the northern part of the Connecticut River have a founding date of sometime in the 1760s. Unlike earlier years, the Upper Valley did not shift gradually northward in location as new settlements appeared to the south.

Common backgrounds had a unifying effect in this period. The majority of the settlers came from Connecticut, as evidenced by the region's many Connecticut town names. Moving into the Upper Valley, they brought with them

rather than the somewhat arbitrary state boundaries being drawn.

Geography helped further define and maintain this Upper Valley identity. North of Massachusetts, the Connecticut River does not pass through rolling hills or flat lands, as it does to the south. Instead, the terrain is generally mountainous, the land rocky. The task of clearing and farming this land was more difficult than the task of clearing Connecticut and Massachusetts land, and the settlers shared that new experience. Geography later affected the development of agriculture, further distinguishing the Upper

shared religious and political beliefs.

Cohesion in the area reached its peak during the Revolutionary War, when a regional rebellion led to an unsuccessful proposal that the Upper Valley towns form a new state called New Connecticut. Two later attempts to make New Hampshire towns in the Upper Valley part of Vermont also failed. Nevertheless, these efforts demonstrate that the valley inhabitants believed they were part of a semiautonomous region, separate from the political and economic center of New Hampshire to the southeast. For many, the Upper Valley defined their lives,

Valley from the lower reaches of the Connecticut River.

Despite these indications that at one time the Upper Valley formed a somewhat cohesive region, it is important to remember that the Upper Valley was never truly independent, nor was its way of life peculiar only to valley towns. Similar isolated hilltop farms dotted most of Vermont, and other areas were equally dependent on a river for transportation. Combined with the many factors that made the Upper Valley a separate and

15

different place were some that worked to undermine regional cohesion. State boundaries, which placed the east bank towns in New Hampshire and the west bank ones in Vermont, prevented the development of political cohesion or autonomy. Differing economic interests also worked against the emergence of a unified Upper Valley. For example, lumbering was more important in the northern reaches of the river than it was in the southern, where locks and canals were built. Conflicts soon arose between these sections regarding the uses of the river.

The chief erosion of regional cohesiveness occurred after turnpikes and railroads replaced the Connecticut as the primary means of transportation. As long as the Upper Valley was dependent on the river for transportation, the area was somewhat unified. Completed in the early 1800s, the first turnpikes broke the region's isolation. They also began to shift commerce away from the valley, toward Concord and Boston. More readily accessible, those cities assumed greater economic importance for the Upper Valley, with the result that for many towns the valley itself lost significance.

Begun by the turnpikes, this process was completed by the railroads. River traffic collapsed completely in the mid-nineteenth century with the arrival of the first trains. At first only business interests were drawn away from the valley, as towns and industries became connected with new, more distant markets. But by the end of the century, the further extension of railroads, combined with newly developed recreational areas such as Lake Sunapee, meant that people also sought leisure activities far away. The orientation away from the valley entered almost every aspect of daily life.

My goal in writing this book has been to recapture some of that common past which continues to exert its influence on the towns situated along the entire course of the Connecticut River between Vermont and New Hampshire. I should perhaps stress *some*, because the book is not meant to be a comprehensive history of the Upper Valley. Most of its chapters first appeared as weekly newspaper articles for the West Lebanon, New Hampshire *Valley News*.

In deciding every week which article to write, I always searched for an event that was somehow typical of earlier life in the valley. The same principle guided me when I wrote about individuals. They are remembered, of course, because of their uniqueness, but in some way each life was also exemplary in relation to the valley's history. Instead of writing a continuous narrative, I have composed a series of vignettes. Arranged chronologically, they highlight broad patterns of historical development in the Upper Valley, as well as provide a sense of the area's flavor and diversity.

A last word on regional cohesion: After all the arguments, this newcomer's recommendation is that his readers take a trip down Interstate 91 into Massachusetts or Connecticut. Remain there a few days, longer if possible, then head north along the river. When you leave Greenfield, Massachusetts behind, when you cross into Vermont and the countryside changes from alluvial flood plain to granite hills, you will know that you are in a new area. The land is different, and, as you drive northward you will sense that its towns and farms share a common history which has shaped them and which continues to bind them together.

The Early Years

BEFORE EUROPEAN DISCOVERY
TO THE 1790s

1

Before European Discovery

A COMMON belief is that the Upper Valley was uninhabited prior to the arrival of European settlers in the 1700s. Long-time residents will say that Indians never lived here because the winters were too harsh. And as recently as 1978, the *Vermont Atlas and Gazetteer* asserted: "Prior to the coming of the white man, the present state of Vermont was largely an uninhabited no-man's land. The entire area was a disputed hunting ground claimed by the Algonquin tribes of Indians, who resided in what is now Canada, and the powerful Iroquois federation, whose principal villages were in what is now New York State."

Despite this and other similar statements, Vermont was not "an uninhabited no-man's land" before the arrival of European settlers. Nor was the northern part of New Hampshire, nor the Upper Valley. Anthropologists and historians have established that the area was most likely inhabited as long as eight thousand years ago. They also believe that native American peoples lived here continuously until the arrival of Europeans.

The first people to enter this region were probably small migratory bands who hunted large game. Over thousands of years various cultural stages evolved — different tools were used, pottery was eventually introduced, as were copper implements, and horticulture was slowly developed. After A.D. 1000 the Indians in northern New England began to coalesce into a small number of large central villages. By 1600 most of New Hampshire and Vermont, as well as a part of Canada and a small part of northern Massachusetts, were inhabited by a group of Indians called the Western Abenaki. The term "Western Abenaki" is essentially a modern linguistic term, denoting a common language spoken by various smaller bands of Indians who lived in the area.

This common language did not, however, provide a larger sense of group identity for the Indians. More important than language were the river drainages, which essentially defined the homelands of the different groups.

The Indians who occupied the Upper Valley were the Sokoki. Their main center of population was at Squakheag (Northfield, Massachusetts), but there were other settlements north along the Connecticut River. Probably their villages were near waterfalls or rapids, where fishing was good. Historians speculate, for example, that Bellows Falls might have been the site of a Sokoki settlement.

Very little is known about the Sokoki and other tribes who inhabited most of the interior of New Hampshire and Vermont, as there are almost no documents which describe Indian life before the arrival of European settlers. The only existing account of the tribes within this area is by the French explorer Samuel de Champlain. After encountering Indians dwelling along the Saco River, Champlain wrote in 1605: "These savages shave off the hair far up on the head, and wear what remains very long, which they comb and twist behind in various ways very neatly, intertwined with feathers which they attach to the head. They paint their faces black and red, like the other savages which we have seen. They are an agile people, with well-formed bodies. Their weapons are pikes, clubs, bows and arrows, at the end of which some attach the tail of a fish called the signoc, others bones, while the arrows of others are entirely of wood. They till and cultivate the soil, something which we have not hitherto observed. In the place of ploughs, they use an instrument of very hard wood, shaped like a spade."

Describing the Indian dwellings along the Saco River, Champlain wrote:

"The forests in the interior are very thin, although abounding in oaks, beaches, ashes, and elms; in wet places there are many willows. The savages dwell permanently in this place, and have a large cabin surrounded by palisades made of rather large trees placed by the side of each other, in which they take refuge when their enemies make war upon them. They cover their cabins with oak bark. This place is very pleasant, and as agreeable as any to be seen. The river is abundant in fish, and is bordered by meadows."

No reports exist prior to 1675 on native American groups living in the area because the first European settlers generally occupied only coastal regions.

The Connecticut River, for example, was first discovered by European explorers in 1614, when the Dutch navigator Adriaen Block explored its lower sixty miles. Prevented by the Enfield Rapids in Connecticut from further exploration, the northern ends of the river remained unknown. The first European settlements were confined to the south, and several years passed before fur traders pushed northward into the Upper Valley. When fur traders and later settlers did enter the Upper Valley, most Indians of the region had been killed by a series of epidemics. The few survivors had largely withdrawn to Canada.

Gordon Day is the foremost historian on the Western Abenaki Indians, and he

Samuel de Champlain's drawing of his 1610 battle with Algonquin Indians against an Iroquois fort. From Les Voyages de Champlain, *Paris, 1613.*

19

Maple sugar and syrup were introduced to Europeans by the Indians.
From J. F. Lafitau, Moeurs des Sauvages Ameriquains, *Paris, 1724.*

has written that the Sokokis, like other groups of Western Abenaki, lived in fairly sizable villages. These were typically located on bluffs, which provided security while keeping the Sokokis near the flat plains below, where they grew corn, beans, and squash. They lived in long houses with arched roofs and covered with bark. A household consisted of one to several nuclear families living together in a single dwelling. A typical town contained twenty or thirty houses with a population of two or three hundred.

In 1605 when Champlain first observed them, the Western Abenaki villages were palisaded for defense. This was several years before the arrival of many French and English explorers, so the defenses were not for protection against Europeans. As historians also believe that the Western Abenaki tribes fought little among themselves, the palisades probably served as defense against the Mohawks who were expanding to the east in search of new hunting grounds.

The Western Abenaki, including the Sokoki, differed from neighboring groups to the north and south in that their culture was based on a mixture of hunting and horticultural activities. Tribes to the north were more fully hunting-and-gathering cultures, and the native peoples in New York and the southern part of New England were more dependent on agriculture. Although the Western Abenaki possibly adopted horticulture as early as five or six hundred years before the arrival of Europeans, it never became their dominant source of food. The short and unpredictable growing season must have precluded such a possibility. Horticulture was apparently adopted only as an important supplement to hunting and gathering, and it was carried out in a way that conformed to the seasonal hunting-and-gathering cycle.

The division of labor in this mixed culture was similar to that of most native American peoples elsewhere. The domain of the men was hunting and fishing, and cultivating crops was the women's responsibility. The one exception was tobacco. Tobacco was generally regarded by native Americans as possessing special powers which facilitated communication with the spirits. Consequently, it was treated differently from ordinary food. It was grown apart from other crops, and the men always tended it.

Crops were, of course, planted in the spring, but the Sokokis' spring agricultural cycle in the Upper Valley began — as ours still does today — with the collection of maple sap. Women collected sap in birchbark containers and clay pots, and maple syrup and sugar were then made by boiling the sap down. Later, Indians introduced maple sugaring to the Europeans. In addition to collecting maple sap at this time, the Sokoki women gathered wild plant foods. The men were occupied in fishing and netting spring flights of passenger pigeons. Some of the fish and pigeons were eaten immediately, but the catches of both were substantial, and much was smoked and stored.

In May the women planted maize, beans, and squash in alluvial fields near their villages. Through the summer they tended those fields, while the men hunted, fished, and traveled. Often the men made trips to large interior lakes for fishing and hunting. The women also gathered berries and fruits, as they ripened through the summer months. Blueberries were especially prized. In late summer nuts were collected, including beechnuts, black walnuts, butternuts, chestnuts, and hickory nuts. Some green corn and beans were also taken in the late summer, but the main harvesting was done by the women in September. After they were picked, the ears of corn were first hung to dry. Then they were shelled, and the corn was stored in bark-lined pits.

In autumn passenger pigeons were again caught during their southward migration. At this time waterfowl and eels were also caught, and many were stored for winter. When hard winter set in, the Western Abenakis returned to their villages. They then made relatively brief trips into interior hunting grounds, depending heavily on stored food during the coldest months. The rich and varied harvest gathered throughout the year largely sustained them through the winter as they awaited spring, when once again maple sap was collected, pigeons and fish were caught, and crops were planted.

In *The Archaeology of New England*, the anthropologist Dean R. Snow estimates that in 1600 there were ten thousand Western Abenaki in New Hampshire, Vermont, and parts of Canada and Massachusetts. He has also estimated that thirty-eight hundred of these Indians inhabited the Upper Valley. These figures are only guesses, and the number of Sokoki and other Western Abenaki Indians may have been considerably higher. But whatever the numbers, by the end of the seventeenth century almost all Sokoki and other groups of Western Abenaki had vanished from New Hampshire and Vermont. The reasons for their disappearance are multiple, but the most pronounced reason was the epidemics which killed a major part of the native American groups in New England. These epidemics began in 1615, resulting from increasingly large European expeditions to America. The native populations of America had virtually no resistance to small pox, measles, and other illnesses, and consequently whole towns and villages were wiped out when these diseases were introduced by Europeans.

Because they were farther north and in the interior, the Sokokis and other Western Abenakis were apparently spared the first epidemic of 1615. In the 1630s, however, their entire population was decimated by sickness. Snow estimates that 98 percent of the Western Abenakis were killed by illnesses introduced by Europeans. Of a possible ten thousand, only two hundred and fifty survived. Such a mortality rate means that fewer than one hundred of the nearly four thousand Sokokis survived.

As a result of continued hostilities with the Iroquois and with the European settlers, the remaining Sokokis and other Western Abenakis gradually abandoned the Upper Valley and other parts of New Hampshire and Vermont. By 1695 many of the Western Abenaki had begun to settle in the village of Odanak on the St. Francis River in the province of Quebec. A mission was established there by the French in 1700, and over the next one hundred years practically all the Indians originally living in New Hampshire, Vermont, western Maine, and the Connecticut Valley in Massachusetts moved to Odanak. In 1759 the village at St. Francis was the site of Major Robert Rogers' well known Indian raid during the Seven Years War.

Descendents of the St. Francis Indians, as these Indians came to be known, live today in Canada. Several other smaller pockets of Western Abenaki also exist in Thetford and Swanton, Vermont, and in parts of New Hampshire. They are all that remain of the Indians who once inhabited the Upper Valley.

FUR TRADE IN THE CONNECTICUT VALLEY

THE SEARCH for furs was what led Adriaen Block to discover the Connecticut River in 1614, and for many years afterward this same search dominated European concern with the Connecticut River Valley. Highly profitable trade networks were established, providing an organized way to obtain furs from an immense territory. For the Indians, however, the fur trade had negative effects, introducing changes which greatly undermined their traditional ways.

The most apparent effect of the fur trade was the spread of disease into the interior regions. In 1633, for example, Captain John Oldham of Massachusetts became the first Englishman to travel overland to the Upper Valley. One of Oldham's purposes in making this trip was to ascertain the region's fur potential. Shortly after his trip to the Upper Valley, there was an outbreak of smallpox in the area. Whether Oldham was actually responsible is not known, but some Indians did blame him.

Another change brought by the fur trade was the use of manufactured cloth among the Indians. In the Connecticut Valley beaver pelts were the major commodity obtained from the Indians, and manufactured cloth was the item most commonly exchanged for the pelts. The

THE FUR TRADERS AT MONTREAL. *Pastel drawing, by G. A. Reid. C-11013 Public Archives Canada.*

reason was simple. It required far less time for an Indian to make clothing from wool or cotton than from hides. Wool or cotton clothing was also more comfortable to wear, especially in humid weather. About four and a half hides per year were needed to clothe each individual. Sufficient clothing of cotton and wool could be obtained in exchange for fewer than four and a half pelts. With the introduction of manufactured cloth, the Indians became increasingly dependent on the Europeans.

European trade with the Indians might have stabilized if the Indians had possessed something other than furs for exchange. Beaver have a low fertility rate, and heavy trapping rapidly depletes their numbers. Confronted with a dwindling supply of beaver, the various tribes were hard pressed to gather sufficient pelts to trade for the European items they now desired and needed. In an attempt to trap more animals, tribes began to extend their traditional hunting grounds. The result was increased warfare among neighboring tribes. In the Upper Valley, for example, the traditional enmity between the Western Abenakis and the Iroquois became increasingly bound up with the fur trade. In 1628 the Iroquois, seeking to extend their hunting grounds, defeated the Sokokis, Mahicans, and others to the east of the Mohawks. For the next forty years the Sokokis were involved in fierce warfare with the Iroquois

— a warfare often connected with British and French attempts to gain control over the fur trade in the Northeast. In the end such tribal wars did little to enhance a particular tribe's control over the declining fur trade. Instead, the fighting only contributed to the decline of Indian populations.

The fur trade had one final detrimental effect on native American groups, coming, ironically, when the fur trade was almost exhausted in the area. Not having sufficient pelts to trade, the Indians found they had nothing to exchange for cloth and other items except their land. William Haviland and Marjory Power point out in *The Original Vermonters* that the fur trade in the Connecticut Valley reached its height in 1654, then began its inevitable decline. By 1656 fur yields were well below average, and in subsequent years they continued to fall. At the same time colonial settlements had grown to the point where land was often in short supply. Consequently, in the 1660s Connecticut Valley traders began to extend credit to the Indians, using their cleared land as collateral. As it was impossible to gather enough pelts to pay for goods already obtained, the land was rapidly transferred to British settlers. With their land gone, the Indians had nothing with which to trade. This did not mean that the Indians simply disappeared, but as a consequence, many years of bitter warfare followed.

Major Robert Rogers' Raid on the St. Francis Indians

ALTHOUGH the Sokoki have never become part of the popular lore about the Upper Valley, Indian stories abound. From 1675 until the 1760s the Upper Valley was largely an unoccupied territory, while the British, French, and Indians were engaged in an almost continuous series of wars. Many skirmishes occurred in the area, and a great number of captives were forced to march northward to Canada through the wilderness of the Upper Valley and Vermont. Over the years tales of these fights and the fate of the captives have been recounted again and again. The tales are interesting, and generally they contain a certain amount of truth. But exaggerations and distortions are also commonplace.

A case in point is Major Robert Rogers' raid on the St. Francis Indians, one of the most famous events of the many years of war in New England. The story of this raid has been told numerous times, the best known reconstruction being Kenneth Robert's novel *Northwest Passage.* The significance of Rogers' raid lay in the supposed fact that it dealt a crushing blow to the St. Francis Indians, bringing an end to the continuous attacks on English settlements. The story is chiefly interesting because of the numerous adventures and hardships experienced by Rogers and his Rangers during and after their raid.

The order for this raid came during the Seven Years War, when the British General Jeffrey Amherst flew into a rage upon learning that two of his officers, traveling under a flag of truce, had been taken captive by St. Francis Indians. The two officers were using the flag of truce as a ruse, to pass through French lines,

but this in no way lessened Amherst's rage. He was determined "to chastise these savages with some severity" for not having honored the flag.

On September 13, 1759, Amherst ordered Rogers to proceed "this night . . . to Missisquey Bay, from whence you will march and attack the enemy's settlements on the south-side of the river St. Lawrence in such a manner as you shall judge most effectual. . . . Remember the barbarities . . . committed by the enemy's Indian scoundrels on every occasion. . . . Take your revenge, but don't forget that tho' those villains have dastardly and promiscuously murdered

MAJOR ROBERT ROGERS. *French mezzotint, probably made during Rogers' lifetime. Courtesy Baker Library.*

2 5

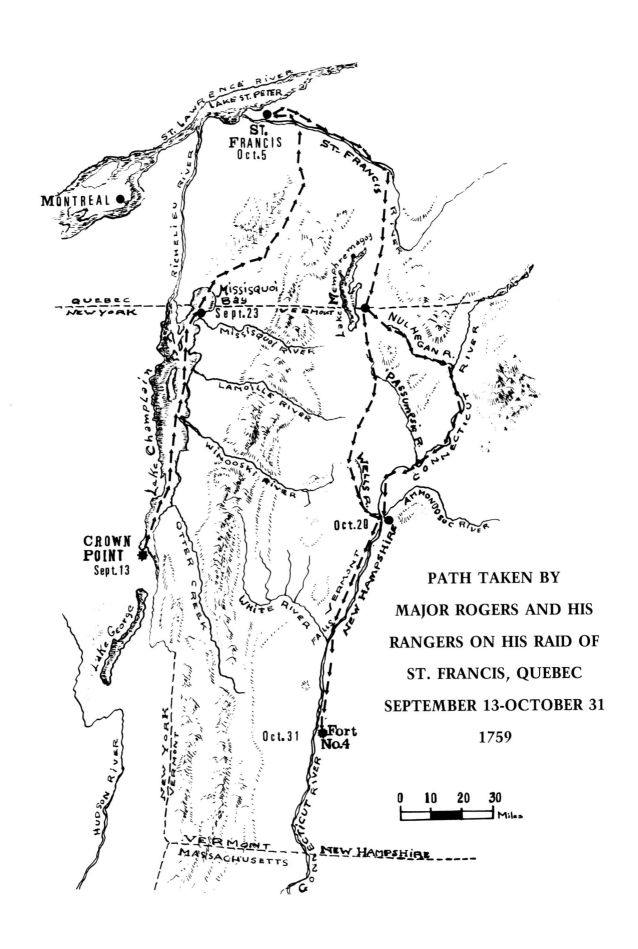

ST. LAWRENCE RIVER

LAKE ST. PETER

ST.
FRANCIS
Oct.5

ST. FRANCIS RIVER

MONTREAL

RICHELIEU RIVER

Lake Memphremagog

QUEBEC
NEW YORK

Missisquoi
Bay
Sept.23

VERMONT

NULHEGAN R.

MISSISQUOI RIVER

LAMOILLE RIVER

PASSUMPSIC R.

CONNECTICUT RIVER

Lake Champlain

WINOOSKI RIVER

WELLS R.

Oct.28

AMMONOOSUC RIVER

OTTER CREEK

CROWN
POINT
Sept.13

Lake George

WHITE RIVER

FALLS

VERMONT
NEW HAMPSHIRE

PATH TAKEN BY
MAJOR ROGERS AND HIS
RANGERS ON HIS RAID OF
ST. FRANCIS, QUEBEC
SEPTEMBER 13-OCTOBER 31
1759

NEW YORK
VERMONT

HUDSON RIVER

Oct.31

Fort
No.4

0   10   20   30
[scale bar] Miles

VERMONT
MASSACHUSETTS

NEW HAMPSHIRE

CONNECTICUT RIVER

the women and children of all ages, it is my orders that no women or children are killed or hurt. . . ." This last statement was apparently for the record, as Amherst showed no displeasure when hearing that women and children had been killed in the raid on St. Francis.

After nightfall that same September 13th, Rogers and two hundred Rangers and friendly Indians embarked from Crown Point on Lake Champlain. They traveled in whaleboats, journeying only at night so as to elude the French patrols on the lake. During these first days of the expedition Rogers and his Rangers encountered various mishaps, including a gunpowder explosion which injured several men. The injured were sent back to Crown Point, as were others who had become sick. After having been out for only six days, Rogers had sent back a fifth of his force. The others continued northward, and early on September 23rd they reached the Missisquoi Bay at the extreme northern end of Lake Champlain. Here they hid their boats and some provisions, then marched northeasterly into the wilderness. According to Rogers' journal, two Indians were left behind "to lie at a distance in sight of the boats, and there to stay until I came back, except the enemy found them; in which case they were with all possible speed to follow on my track."

After two days of marching, these two Indians caught up with Rogers to report that a force of four hundred French had discovered the boats, and that half the French force was now in pursuit of the Rangers. With their provisions captured and an enemy force behind them, Rogers realized he would have to return by way of the Connecticut River. To insure that this might be possible, he sent back a small group of Rangers to Crown Point, requesting that Amherst send provisions up the Connecticut River from Fort No. 4 to the Wells River, "that being the way I should return, if at all. . . ."

The Rangers continued their march through the wilderness, walking for nine days through a spruce bog. Not daring to light fires, they could never dry their clothing or warm themselves. They slept on spruce boughs laced together in the trees above bog water. Finally the ground became firm, and a short distance beyond they stood at the St. Francis River. Fording this, they marched fifteen miles downstream until they were within striking distance of the village of St. Francis. On October 5, 1759, Rogers and two officers moved forward to reconnoiter the village, where they observed the Indians "in a high frolic or dance."

At three o'clock the next morning Rogers moved his small army of 141 men to within fifteen hundred yards of the village. They waited until a half hour before dawn, then, at a signal from Rogers, they attacked. According to Rogers, the attack was a complete surprise and within a short time the village had been burned and most of the Indians killed. Rogers estimated that two hundred died in the attack. Of the Rangers, only one Stockbridge Indian was killed and seven were wounded. The only thing remaining at the village of St. Francis were three houses, which Rogers spared because they held provisions, including some corn. The Rangers divided the corn and began the march back immediately.

The journey homeward was worse than the long nights slogging through bogs. The Rangers needed to travel one hundred miles just to bypass Lake Memphremagog on their way to the Connecticut River. The early autumn weather turned cold, and for the first eight days there was freezing rain. Soon the few provisions taken at St. Francis were gone. Despite exhaustion and hunger, the Rangers marched as rapidly as possible through mountain wilderness, not daring to stop to rest or to build a fire for warmth. The French and Indians were in close pursuit. After eight days the Rangers decided somewhere near Lake Memphremagog to split into smaller parties, hoping that they might come upon game. Some of these groups were soon found by the pursuing French, and several Rangers were killed. Rogers' group had the least difficulty, although all his men were weakened by fatigue, the cold, and lack of food.

In the middle of October, Rogers and his group reached the junction of the Passumpsic and Connecticut Rivers. From here they hurried south toward the Wells River, where they hoped to find the supplies requested from Amherst. As they approached the Wells River on October 20, 1759, they heard shots in the distance. Assuming this to be the relief party, Rogers fired several answering shots. With renewed hope the men hastened forward, but at Wells River they found only the embers of a fire and no provisions.

Amherst had ordered Lieutenant Samuel Stevens to proceed to Wells River with a small party and to wait there until he was certain Rogers was not returning. Because of potential dangers, Stevens decided to camp three or four miles south of Wells River. He and some of his small party traveled daily to the river and fired their guns as signals. There is confusion as to what happened on October 20, whether Stevens heard Rogers' answering shots or whether he thought his group was about to come under attack. That day, however, Stevens decided to return to Fort No. 4, taking the provisions with him. Stevens was later court-martialed for his actions.

Having no food, the Rangers despaired. "Our distress upon this occasion was truly inexpressible," Rogers wrote in his journal. "Our spirits, greatly depressed by the hunger and fatigue we had already suffered, now almost sunk within us, seeing no resource left, nor any reasonable ground to hope that we should escape a most miserable death by famine." Still, Rogers did not give up. He set the men to digging up groundnuts and lily roots, and a raft was made from dry pine logs. With two other Rangers and a captive Indian boy, Rogers then began a harrowing journey down the Connecticut River, promising to return in ten days with provisions.

Unfortunately, the raft broke up at the rapids above the White River Falls, and the four men barely managed to get ashore. They began to make a second raft, yet "not being able to cut down trees, [they] burnt them down, and then burnt them off at proper lengths." They rode this raft to Fort No. 4, arriving on October 31. Within a half hour after Rogers' arrival at the fort, provisions were sent up the Connecticut to the Rangers at Wells River. The provisions arrived four days later, exactly ten days after Rogers had begun his journey down the Connecticut. After a short rest Rogers also returned northward to Wells River "to seek and bring in as many of our men as I can find. . . ." Of the 141 men who had participated in the St. Francis raid, 3 officers and 46 sergeants and privates did not return.

These are the details of the St. Francis raid, as recounted by Rogers himself in his journals. Every retelling or reenactment of this story has been based on Rogers' account, but over the years the simplicity of Rogers' journal entries has been blown into something much larger. In the novel *Northwest Passage* and elsewhere, the raid on St. Francis has been portrayed as one of the most exciting adventures of the period, as well as one of the most significant because it crushed the St. Francis Indians.

Doubt has always existed about this popular view of the St. Francis raid. Basis for the doubt rests on the fact that the French, who were in St. Francis immediately after the attack, reported only thirty casualties, instead of the two hundred estimated by Rogers. The discrepancy in these two reports could not be explained, but it has been assumed that the French numbers must be more reliable, as they were based on an actual count. Recently the historian Gordan Day uncovered evidence which tends to support the French report of thirty casualties. Through numerous talks with present-day residents of St. Francis, Day learned of two family oral traditions which recall events in the lives of ancestors who lived over four generations ago. Included in each was a story of the St. Francis raid.

According to both stories, the Indians of St. Francis were warned of an impending attack by a Mahican, who was a stranger. As Rogers was accompanied by some Mahicans, one of these could very well have warned the Indians. Warned, most of the villagers hid elsewhere when the Rangers attacked. The fight was short, and the village burned to the ground. Rogers no doubt assumed that most of the St. Francis Indians had perished inside their houses from fire, which would explain his high estimate of two hundred killed.

That only thirty Indians, and not two hundred, were killed in the raid on St. Francis greatly alters the significance of this well-known expedition. If so few were killed at St. Francis, the claim of a major military victory has no basis. The order for the raid on St. Francis had no real military objective. Instead, Amherst ordered the mission as revenge for the capture of his two officers who were misusing the flag of truce. Lacking a wider military purpose, the order to attack St. Francis appears irresponsible, as it unnecessarily exposed Rogers and his small army to extremely harsh conditions in the wilderness and to numerous dangers. In the end it also appears that the raid may have taken the lives of more Rangers than Indians.

Disappointment at Wells River. Courtesy National Life of Vermont.

FORT NO. 4

PRIOR TO 1738, Massachusetts lay claim to much of what is now New Hampshire. Wishing to protect its northwestern frontier and hoping in particular to solidify its claims in the more northern stretches of the Connecticut River valley, it granted four townships there under the designations No. 1, No. 2, No. 3, and No. 4 — today the towns of Chesterfield, Westmoreland, Walpole, and Charlestown.

The first settlers came to No. 4 in 1740 and began to clear land. For the first few years no attacks were made on No. 4, but in 1743 rumors circulated about an impending war between France and England. Deciding to take measures for their defense, the settlers voted on November 24, 1743, to erect a fort. Possibly built under the direction of Colonel John Stoddard, the fort was in the form of a square. Each side was 180 feet in length, and the walls were made of large squared timbers laid in the manner of a log cabin. A stockade fence twelve feet high stood to the north, east, and west sides. Within the enclosure were six buildings called province houses, six connecting lean-tos, and a watch tower connected to a building called the Great Chamber. These structures, placed directly against the walls of the fort, were reinforced on every side. Consequently, if any enemy succeeded in entering the fort enclosure, the buildings could still serve as places of defense.

Great Britain declared war against France and Spain in March 1744, but No. 4 remained unmolested for two years. Then, on April 19, 1746, a party of forty French and Indians ambushed and captured three No. 4 settlers returning from their saw mill. Repeated raids were made on the settlement, and at the end of the summer of 1746, No. 4 was abandoned.

No. 4 was particularly vulnerable to attacks because of its isolated position. The northernmost settlement on the Connecticut, it lay some fifty miles away from the nearest New Hampshire town. There were no English settlements to the north and west. No. 4 was also situated on the routes traveled by the French and Indians as they approached the English frontier from Canada. One of these routes was by the St. Francis River through Lake Memphremagog, where portage was then made to the Passumsic River. This was followed to its juncture with the Connecticut at present-day Barnet. Another route

Sketch for Fort No. 4 restoration. Courtesy Martha Frizzell,
SECOND HISTORY OF CHARLESTOWN, N.H., *Littleton, N.H., 1955.*

led to the White River, then down the Connecticut. The route most frequently traveled by the Indians was up Otter Creek and over the mountains to the Black River. But no matter what route was chosen, the Connecticut was always the final junction. And there lay No. 4.

The fort at No. 4 was reoccupied shortly after its abandonment, when, in March 1747, Captain Phineas Stevens returned with thirty men. The fort came under repeated attack, but it remained secure until peace was declared in 1748. However, the official peace did not end the attacks on No. 4. Sporadic Indian attacks continued, and the few settlers there maintained dwellings within the confines of the fort. In 1753, No. 4 was chartered by New Hampshire as the town of Charlestown, and during the same year raids against the fort seemed to cease.

The settlers hoped a permanent peace had been achieved, but the absence of attacks proved to be only a lull in the fighting. In 1754 the British and French were engaged in what became called the Seven Years War. Among the defenders at Charlestown was a detachment of Rangers.

In 1759 Quebec fell to the British, and in 1760 Montreal was captured, bringing the Seven Years War to an end in North America. A peace treaty was signed in 1763, but by then settlers were already pushing north of Charlestown into the Upper Valley. After years of warfare the fort was no longer needed, and in 1763 the town records mention it for the last time. That year it was voted to build a new meeting house "on the grade where the fort stood." The fort vanished until its reconstruction began in the early 1960s.

The Age of Self-Sufficient Farming

IN THE 1760s almost the entire Upper Valley was rapidly transformed from a wilderness into a settled frontier. Hostilities with the French and Indians were at an end, making the area safe for the first time in almost a hundred years. And although there still remained territorial disputes between New Hampshire and New York, Governor Benning Wentworth's land grants opened the Upper Valley to settlement.

The early settlers in the Upper Valley and other parts of the hill country in Vermont and New Hampshire were extremely optimistic about their chances. The climate was harsh and the terrain rocky and hilly, but the soil was known to be fertile, and fish and game were abundant. The area had great agricultural promise, it was firmly believed, if only a farmer

worked hard to clear and cultivate the wooded land. In part the optimism of the settlers was not unwarranted. When the land was first cleared, the newly created fields were covered with "a thick stratum of vegetable mould" left by the centuries-long growth of forest. As long as this thick humus remained, bountiful crops could be grown, even on the poorer uplands. Unfortunately, this rich layer of top soil was rapidly used up or washed away, resulting in a dramatic decrease of per-acre output.

If a part of the settlers' optimism was based on the reality of a rich soil, another part had a footing only in wishful thinking. A widespread sentiment among the early settlers, for example, was that the winters were growing milder every year. In 1809 Samuel Williams even wrote in his *Natural and Civil History of Vermont*: "As soon as it [the snow] is melted upon the mountains, the earth appears to be greatly fertilized." If snow were indeed considered a fertilizer, then the upland hill towns buried in snow up to one hundred inches must have been thought to be the most fertile of all the land.

Believing the area to be bountiful, settlers moved to the Upper Valley and Vermont in sizable numbers, especially in the years after the Revolutionary War. The town of Orford, for example, increased from a population of 376 in 1786 to 988 in the year 1800. In 1830 over 1,800 people were living there. Similar dramatic increases in population occurred in many other Upper Valley towns, including Walpole, Keene, Lebanon, and Lyme in New Hampshire, and Thetford, Norwich, and Royalton in Vermont. In fact, the same sizable increase in population occurred throughout the entire state of Vermont during this period. In 1781, Vermont had an estimated population of 30,000. Ten years later the federal census showed the population had increased to 85,000. By 1810, it was 217,000.

Despite the considerable optimism which brought the increasing numbers of settlers into the area, life in this early period was not easy. Even before a family could move, a few seasons' work was necessary to make the land ready for settlement. A man almost always came first, unaccompanied by wife or children. Upon arrival — usually in the spring or early summer — he began immediately to clear a part of his land and to construct some kind of shelter. One season's work was usually not enough. The man often returned to work a second summer, after spending the autumn and winter with his family. Sometimes even more than two years were required before the land was sufficiently cleared and prepared. The first settler in Norwich, Vermont, Samuel Slafter, spent four consecutive summers working his land before finally bringing his family to their pioneer home.

A woman's work was greatly increased when her husband was away

Clearing the land. From Orsamus Turner, PIONEER HISTORY. . . . *Buffalo, 1850.*

clearing land. In addition to her numerous household chores, she now had to do everything her husband normally did. This included watching after crops and livestock on the farm which the family intended soon to leave.

When a part of the land was at last cleared enough to plant a first crop, the settler and his family moved northward, often traveling during the coldest winter months when they could move over the frozen Connecticut River. Other settlers came in spring, journeying in log canoes. There existed no passable roads for wagons to the Upper Valley. The first years were exhausting ones, filled with toil and sometimes discouraging hardships. The most difficult task was the further clearing of land. Underbrush was cleared and larger timber destroyed, usually by cutting and burning. The ashes were converted to potash, which could be sold for soap and glassmaking. Later, often after the first harvest, stones and boulders were moved to the sides of the fields. Clearing the land was a slow process. On the average from one to three acres were cleared by a settler each year. After ten years of labor most farmers had no more than fifteen cleared acres, although some — with several grown sons — had as many as fifty to eighty cleared acres.

The first housing of the settlers was usually quite crude and not comfortable. Jeremy Belknap wrote in his *History of New Hampshire*: ''They erect a square of poles, notched at the ends to keep them fast together. The crevices are plastered with clay or the stiffest earth which can be had, mixed with moss or straw. The roof is either bark or split boards. The chimney a pile of stones; within which a fire is made on the ground, and a hole is left in the roof for the smoke to pass out. Another hole is made in the side of the house for a window, which is occasionally closed with a wooden shutter!'' Most settlers lived in these first, crude houses for ten to fifteen years, some even longer.

In the first years the settlers could not depend on their own wheat and corn

Ten years later. From Turner's PIONEER HISTORY.

to provide them with all the food they needed. Twenty bushels an acre was an average crop in New Hampshire, but there were few cleared acres in the first years. Consequently, settlers foraged for nuts and berries, and hunted and fished to supplement what they raised. What they found in the forest were welcome additions to their usual drab staples.

All of these early farms were generally self-sufficient. Almost everything used or consumed — including clothing, food, and household items like soap — was made or raised by the settlers. To succeed in this endeavor, the work performed by both the man and the woman was essential. The division of labor on Vermont and New Hampshire hill farms followed the traditional patterns of European settlers in America. Clearing the land and raising crops and livestock generally defined the man's work sphere. All chores and tasks connected with the household represented the woman's province. This division was not always strict, especially in the early years of settlement, when women often helped their husbands with clearing and planting.

In comparison with what we do today, the chores performed by both men and women were enormous. They usually arose well before sunrise and worked to sunset or later. In summer the man's work took him daily into the fields, where he planted wheat and corn. Haying was another summer chore, and, whenever possible, new land was cleared. In the relatively inactive autumn and early winter months, wheat was thrashed. Whatever domestic animals a settler had — cows, sheep, pigs — needed daily tending, and buildings and fences were often either enlarged or repaired.

Preparing and spinning wool into yarn and then weaving cloth was one of the most important and time-consuming jobs performed by women. It was highly skilled work, crucial to the settlers' survival on the isolated, hillside farms of the Upper Valley. Preparing meals was another important task performed by the women. The early settlers' diet was gen-

Twenty years later. From Turner's Pioneer History.

erally simple and often monotonous. There were bean porridges and hasty puddings (a mush made of corn meal), as well as a considerable amount of game. Turnips were the most common vegetable, and maple sugar was the only sweet. Coffee and tea were practically unknown to the settler. Although the food was simple, its preparation was not. To cook required the use of fire. In an age before matches, the steady maintenance of burning embers was no minor task. Equally challenging was the perpetuation of a yeast supply. The yeast might first come from the foam on top of fermenting ale or beer, or perhaps from a piece of saved bread dough. The yeast needed to be continuously maintained, for if its natural growth were interrupted it was difficult to restart.

When the hill country was first settled, the uplands were almost always preferred to low-lying valley locations. According to Harold F. Wilson in *The Hill Country of Northern New England*: "The narrow valleys were often subject to destructive spring floods and to severe freshets after heavy rainstorms, while the land along the streams was apt to be swampy. Beavers had built dams across them, and these obstructions held back the water, often flooding areas which later on became dry and cultivable." Only after the tangled forest growth was removed, exposing the land to the sun and wind, did the lower valley areas finally become dry enough for planting.

The first settlers, accordingly, moved into higher elevations, where the land was dry and more readily cultivable. The forest growth was also sparser there, making it easier to clear. Another consideration was the fact that stumps in the fields decayed sooner at higher and dryer elevations than they did on the lower, wetter lands. The hilltops were also less vulnerable to early frosts.

Because these farms were largely self-sufficient, early settlers were not concerned about convenient access to other settlements. Consequently, the first roads were generally built along the

Sixty years later. From Turner's PIONEER HISTORY.

straightest routes, as this was cheaper than constructing roads through circuitous valleys where bridges might also have had to be be built. Climbing steep hills, even though slow with horse and wagon, did not bother the early settler, whose trips to town were infrequent. Only later, when farming became dependent on the transportation of goods to distant markets, did the inaccessibility of the hillside farms become a problem.

Early farm families also gave little thought to the contour of the land. Farmers produced small amounts, and crops were harvested with sickle and scythe. It made little difference whether the land was rocky or flat or on an incline. Only when farming became fully market oriented, requiring that a few cash crops be grown in large quantities, did the farmers find hillside locations unsuitable. When machinery was later introduced, a rocky, hillside terrain was even less advantageous.

The early settlers saw none of these future disadvantages inherent in the countryside of the Upper Valley and other parts of the hill country. Attracted by the fertility of the land, they migrated to the area in ever-increasing numbers through the end of the eighteenth century and into the first part of the nineteenth. No mention of distant problems could have stopped them. Nor was their eagerness lessened by the hardships they knew they would encounter. For although the life they first lived as settlers was difficult, moving always brought with it the possibility of greatly improving one's life. In 1809 Samuel Williams optimistically wrote in his *History of Vermont*: "Amidst the hard living and hard labor that attends the forming a new settlement, the settler has the most flattering prospects and encouragements. . . . When he comes to apply his labor to his own land, the produce of it becomes extremely profitable. The first crop of wheat will fully pay him for all the expense he has been at, in clearing up, sowing, and fencing his land; and at the same time, increases the value of the land, eight or ten times the original cost. In this way, every day's labor spent in clearing up his land, receives high wages in the grain which it procures, and adds at the same time a quantity of improved land to the farm. . . . This double kind of wages, nature with great benevolence and design, has assigned to the man of industry, when he is first making a settlement in the uncultivated parts of America: And in two or three years, he acquires a very comfortable and independent subsistence for a family, derived from no other source but the earth, and his own industry.''

Carding and spinning wool. From Benjamin Chase, History of Old Chester, N.H., From 1719 to 1869, *Auburn, N.H., 1869.*

The last up-and-down saw mill in Chelsea, Vermont. This saw mill operated until 1897 and was still standing in 1910. Courtesy Chelsea Historical Society.

SAW MILLS AND GRIST MILLS

As soon as possible, settlers built saw mills and grist mills along the streams and rivers. Both were necessities for early farming settlements. The saw mill cut lumber for houses and other buildings; the grist mill ground harvested grain. The early saw and grist mills were extremely small, and were not connected with later industrial development in the Upper Valley and elsewhere in northern New England. They were an integral part of farm life, insuring the existence of the self-sufficient farms.

Saw mills and grist mills could be found along flowing water in almost every community. They needed relatively

The miller. Courtesy Vermont Historical Society.

little power for operation and were usually located at less major waterfalls. In Lebanon, New Hampshire, for example, the first saw and grist mills were built in what became known as West and East Lebanon (where the Mascoma River flows out of Mascoma Lake).

As long as self-sufficient farming remained dominant in the Upper Valley, saw and grist mills were omnipresent. In the nineteenth century, however, farming was gradually transformed into a market-oriented operation, and industrial development made its first appearance. As the self-sufficient farm became a thing of the past, the many saw and grist mills dotting the countryside were slowly abandoned, though they persisted here and there into the early twentieth century.

The Founding of Dartmouth College

V OX CLAMANTIS IN DESERTO — a voice crying in the wilderness. This is the motto of Dartmouth College, and in the early years of settlement the college must have appeared to many in the Upper Valley as a singular voice of civilization. A dense and overgrown forest dotted with independent farms formed the general landscape of the region. Into this wilderness came Eleazar Wheelock, founder of Dartmouth College.

According to Dartmouth's charter, Wheelock's purpose in founding the college was "for the education and instruction of Youth of the Indian Tribes in this land in reading, writing and all parts of Learning which shall appear necessary and expedient for civilizing and christianizing Children of Pagans as well as in all liberal Arts and Sciences; and also English Youth and any others." Reading these words, many people assume that Wheelock hoped to establish Dartmouth College among the Indians, where he might educate them more easily. But this was not the case. Few Indians remained in the Upper Valley when Dartmouth was founded in 1769, and the college had little to do with "the education and instruction of Youth of the Indian Tribes." The "any others" also received little attention, especially if women are included in this category. Dartmouth College admitted primarily "English [male] Youth."

Wheelock's intentions were not as openly hypocritical as that statement implies. Although Dartmouth was to instruct and train white students, it was Wheelock's plan that upon graduation many of those students would become teachers and missionaries to the Indians. Indirectly, Dartmouth College would contribute to the education and "civilization" of the Indians. The decision to "educate" Indians in this oblique manner was not arbitrary. Before the founding of Dartmouth, Wheelock had tried for over twenty years to establish a school for Indians. His efforts had met with only minimal success, and he had grown disillusioned in his once firm belief that Indians could be most successfully educated by removing them from their native environment. Far better, he now thought, to train white missionaries who would go out among the Indians.

Wheelock's concern with educating Indians was an outgrowth of his ministerial duties and his involvement with the Great Awakening, a revivalist movement which swept through New England in two waves — once in the mid-1730s and then more violently in the early 1740s. Born in 1711, Wheelock entered Yale in 1729, where he studied theology. Upon graduation in 1735, he began a pastoral career in Lebanon, Connecticut. From the moment Wheelock began preaching in Lebanon he was convinced that the town — and in fact the entire colony of Connecticut — was spiritually dead. He was determined to change this, and his opportunity came with the Great Awakening. An estimated twenty-five to fifty thousand people were converted during this period, and the religious fervor of Wheelock's preaching was responsible for a considerable number of conversions.

The high-pitched emotionalism of the Great Awakening soon dissipated, leaving evangelists such as Wheelock without a clear sense of religious purpose. For Wheelock, Indians provided a new direction. As Leon Richardson has sug-

ELEAZAR WHEELOCK. *Oil on canvas, by Joseph Steward. Courtesy the Hood Museum of Art.*

gested in his *History of Dartmouth College*, "If the whites were temporarily insensitive to the call of religion, perhaps something might be done with the Indians." And something was done, which eventually culminated in the founding of Dartmouth College.

But back in 1743 Wheelock had no thoughts of a college. In fact, in this first year after the Great Awakening, Wheelock was not even certain what attention to give the Indians. He only knew, as he later wrote, that he felt "in behalf of the poor, savage, perishing creatures like a covetous, craving beggar, as though I could not tell them when to ha' done, or how to leave begging for them, till the Great Design of their being brought to Christ be accomplished." Wheelock was still uncertain what to do, when a young Indian named Samson Occom came to him seeking an education.

Samson Occom was a Mohegan Indian, born in Connecticut sometime in 1723. In an account of his early years, Occom wrote: "I was Born a Heathen in Mmoyouheeunnuck alias Mohegan in N. London-North America. My parents were altogether Heathens, and I was Educated by them in their Heathenish Notions, tho' there was a Sermon Preach'd to our Mohegan Tribe Some times. . . ." In the same account Occom wrote: "My Parents in particular Were very Strong in the Customs of their fore Fathers, and they led a wandering Life up and down in the Wilderness, for my Father was a great Hunter, thus I liv'd with them, till I was Sixteen years old, and then there was a great Stir of Religion in these Parts of the World both amongst the Indians as Well as the English. . . . And when I was Seventeen years of Age I receiv'd a Hope. . . ."

Occom was the first Indian accepted by Wheelock for an education, and the four years they spent together — from 1743 to 1747 — were an extraordinary success. The religious excitement Occom mentions was the revivalist movement of the Great Awakening. Swept up by the fervor of this movement, Occom converted to Christianity. His short account concludes, "And as I began to think about Religion So I began to learn to read, tho' I went to no School, till I was in my nineteenth year, and then I went to the Revd Mr. Wheelocks to learning, and spent four years there. . . ."

Occom hoped to continue his studies and to attend Yale, but problems with his eyes forced him to abandon this goal. Foregoing further education, he became in 1749 a preacher and teacher among the Montauks on Long Island. Through Wheelock's help, this undertaking was sanctioned by the Church of England. Ten years later, again with Wheelock's aid, Occom was ordained a preacher by the Presbyterian Church.

The success achieved with Occom greatly inspired Wheelock. Certain he could educate Indians, Wheelock asked the New Jersey missionary John Brainerd to send two Delawares for his care. The two, Wheelock wrote, "left all their relations and acquaintance, and came alone, on foot, above two hundred miles, thru' a country in which they knew not one mortal, and where they had never passed before, to throw themselves for an education upon a stranger, of whom they had never heard but by Mr. Brainerd." The two arrived in Lebanon, Connecticut, on December 18, 1754.

The arrival of these two Delawares marked the beginning of what became known as Moor's School or Moor's Charity School. The name derives from Colonel Joshua More, a Connecticut farmer, who in 1755 deeded the school two acres of land and a few buildings. Wheelock was pleased with the development of his new charges. A year and a half after their arrival, he wrote that they were well-behaved and contented and that they "read well, have learnt the Assemblies Shorter Catechism thru with the proofs, and have made some entrance into the lattin tongue. They appear seriously inclined for their salvation." Despite Wheelock's enthusiasm, all did not go well. The older youth fell ill in 1756, and in November of that year was sent home. Two months later he died. It was a setback for Wheelock, but he saw no failure.

He concluded that "special care respecting their diet" was necessary, as well as "more exercise." Wheelock continued to accept new pupils, and by the end of 1765 twenty-nine boys had been enrolled in his school for longer or shorter periods.

Basic to the establishment of Moor's School was Wheelock's conviction that Indians could best be educated if removed from their native surroundings. Here they would be free from the evil example of traders or the lure of the hunt, warfare, and wandering. Within the religious environment of Lebanon, Indian boys and girls (girls later also attended the school) would be trained for missionary work among their own tribes. In time these "educated" Indians such as Occom would accomplish far more than white missionaries, as the unconverted Indians would be less prejudiced against them. So reasoned Wheelock in part.

But over the next fifteen years Wheelock achieved nothing which compared to the success he had had with his first pupil. Although some of his Indian pupils did eventually go out as missionaries among the tribes of the Six Nations, their success in "civilizing" and educating other Indians was minimal. In 1763, nine years after he had begun the school, Wheelock wrote: "The most melancholy part of the account I have here to relate . . . has been the bad conduct and behavior of such have been educated here after they left the school, and been put into business abroad: and it is that from which, I think, I had the fullest evidence that a *greater proportion of English youths must be fitted for missionaries.*"

Wheelock's lack of success at Moor's School was not surprising. In the eighteenth century the education of Indians generally meant their conversion to Christianity. The education Indians received was in large measure meant to aid them in their conversion — a point which explains why schools for Indians were established in America long before they were for women and blacks. The conversion to Christianity was also usually accompanied by "civilizing,"

which meant training Indians in the ways and manners of European life.

Moor's School was no exception. Wheelock saw his goal as civilizing the Indians and teaching them "Knowledge of the only true God and Savior." In this way they would be "made good Members of Society, and peacible and quiet Neighbours." To achieve his goal Wheelock instructed his Indian pupils in accordance with eighteenth-century English notions of a good education. Great stress was placed on the "classics," and Indians at the Moor School were taught not only English, but Latin and Greek as well. Wheelock wrote of two Indian pupils that they "will now read Tully, Virgil, and the Greek Testament very handsomely." Such knowledge was valueless in teaching Indians how to live productive lives within the Anglo-Saxon communities or how to educate other Indians to do so.

The curriculum was not the only reason for the project's failure. Wheelock's arrangement of the school day itself weakened the Indians' desire to learn. Unused to strictly regimented days and often suffering from undernourishment, the Indian youths at Moor's School were suddenly subjected to excessively long hours. As Wheelock wrote in his narratives, the Indian pupils were obliged "to be clean and decently dressed, and to be ready to attend prayers before sun-rise in the fall and winter, and at 6 o'clock in the summer." Instruction was from nine to noon, and again from two until five o'clock. "Evening prayer is attended before the daylight is gone. Afterwards they apply to their studies, etc."

Despite mounting disappointment, Wheelock was determined to carry out his plan to send missionaries among the Indians. To start a new phase in this effort, Wheelock turned to Occom. In 1761 Occom left the Montauks and undertook for Wheelock a mission to the Oneidas, in the province of New York. In 1762 Occom made a second visit to the Oneidas, remaining until the outbreak of Pontiac's War in 1763. Wheelock continued sending missionaries to New York until 1768.

In total, he sent nine white missionaries and about fourteen Indian ones. Most met with little success.

Despite Wheelock's desire to give new direction to his Indian Charity School, he might never have done so had it not been for a substantial amount of money received from England. By 1764 Moor's School had been operating for ten years with a yearly attendance of fifteen to twenty Indians. Although firmly established, its various sources of income were insufficient to cover expenses. In 1760 an English friend had written Wheelock, "Had I a converted Indian scholar that could preach and pray in English, something might be done to purpose." Another friend wrote in 1764, "Would it not be best to send Mr. Occom with another Person home a begging? An Indian minister in England might get a Bushel of Money for the School. . . ." Wheelock agreed, and it was arranged to send Occom and Reverend Nathaniel Whitaker, a friend of Wheelock's, to England.

Occom and Whitaker sailed on December 23, 1765, arriving in London on February 6, 1766. Here they remained a few days, "Conceil'd" as Occom wrote, while preparations were made for their first public appearance. On February 10 they met with Lord Dartmouth, and on February 16 Occom preached for the first time in England "to a great Multitude of People." For two years Occom traveled and preached with Whitaker throughout Great Britain. Almost everywhere they went they met with success, due largely to Occom. As time passed, those associated with the fund raising became more trustful of Occom, while they grew less certain about Whitaker. When Occom and Whitaker returned to New England in the spring of 1768, they had raised approximately 11,000 pounds — the largest amount of money ever raised for an American institution in Great Britain before the Revolutionary War.

While Occom was traveling and preaching throughout England, raising money — he thought — to be used in the education of Indians, changes were occur-

The founding of Dartmouth College, 1770. In the open air Eleazar Wheelock offered morning and evening prayers. Woodcut by Samuel E. Brown, in John W. Barber, The History and Antiquities of New England, New York, and New Jersey, *Worcester, Mass., 1841.*

ring in Moor's School in Lebanon, Connecticut. In 1766 Wheelock began accepting white boys in increasing numbers, and by 1768 the number of Indian students began to decline. In January 1769, the father of an Oneida boy came to Lebanon and took his son and five others of the tribe home, leaving only three Indians as students. This was shortly before the school's move to Hanover, N.H.

the teaching of Indians to the teaching of whites.

The many changes made at Moor's School during the two-year trip to England had a profound effect upon Occom. After his return to Connecticut in 1768, he was a different man. Most of his life he had received guidance from Wheelock, but now he grew skeptical of Wheelock's intentions. He refused to set-

This is the earliest view of Dartmouth College. Josiah Dunham, THE MASSACHUSETTS MAGAZINE, *February 1793.*

The one thing certain about the reasons for Wheelock's move from Connecticut to New Hampshire is that the move provided him with an opportunity to alter almost completely the educational goals of Moor's School. Ostensibly, the move was simply to be a physical relocation. In the end the name was changed, the school became a college, and the educational emphasis shifted from

tle in the wilderness among the Iroquois, as Wheelock advocated, and to serve there as a missionary. He also grew increasingly distrustful of Wheelock's plans for the use of the money raised in England. When Wheelock founded Dartmouth College, Occom saw his worst suspicions confirmed — the cause of the Indians had been abandoned for the educational interests of the whites. On July

24, 1771, Occom wrote to Wheelock: "I verily thought once that your Institution was Intended Purely for the poor Indians — with this thought I Cheerfully Ventured my Body & Soul, left my Country my poor young family all my Friends and Relations, to sail over the Boisterous Seas to England, to help forward your School. . . . But when we got Home behold all the glory had Decayed. . . ." Although Occom later wrote to Wheelock in a more reconciliatory tone, the two men never met again. Wheelock did invite Occom to Hanover, and Occom spoke of coming, but he never did.

The English trustees of the funds raised in Great Britain immediately objected to various provisions in the Dartmouth charter, including the fact that money raised to educate Indian boys and girls would now be used for other ends. Wheelock responded to these objections by asserting that although the Dartmouth charter incorporated the school with the college, jurisdiction over the college remained separate from jurisdiction over the school and its funds. He theoretically maintained Moor's School as a semi-autonomous institution. The English trustees finally accepted these assurances, but cautioned Wheelock to keep distinct the expenses of the Moor's Charity School and Dartmouth College — something Wheelock never did.

To assure the continuation of funds from England, Wheelock actively re-cruited some Indians for Dartmouth College. In 1771 there were five Indians enrolled, and, during the decade before Wheelock's death in 1779, a small number of other Indians attended the college. But as in Connecticut, Wheelock had little success in educating these Indians.

His plan to train whites at Dartmouth College to be missionaries among the Indians likewise met with little success. Wheelock had planned to accept a number of whites as "charity students." In return for their educations these students pledged to work for a time as Indian missionaries. In 1772 there were already twenty whites on charity at the college, and over the years there were many more. Some of these men performed service as missionaries, but upon completion of their education many refused to serve.

In 1772 Wheelock had written to Samson Occom that the Indians were: "the first object of the charter. These lands are all given for that purpose, and will so be used for them as long as there shall be Indians upon the continent to partake of that benefit." Wheelock maintained this sentiment to his death, but it was a pledge he could not keep. In 1778 only four Canadian Indians were enrolled at the college, and after Wheelock's death in 1779 the education of Indians became even less important to the school.

Rebellion in the Upper Valley

IT IS ALMOST forgotten today, but there was a time — before Vermont was an entity — when the Upper Valley towns attempted to secede from New Hampshire. Their first goal was to form the state of New Connecticut, and if they had succeeded they most certainly would have forced a permanent unity on the Upper Valley. The Upper Valley would have been a separate state, its boundaries absolutely drawn.

The origins of the rebellion lay in the early settlement patterns of the area. When the original New Hampshire grant was issued, it did not include the Upper Valley. Nor was the valley included in subsequent grants which enlarged New Hampshire. In fact, it was not until July 20, 1764, that an order of the King in Council declared the western bank of the Connecticut River to mark the western boundary of New Hampshire.

Some of western New Hampshire and all of what is now Vermont was for many years disputed territory, claimed by Massachusetts, New Hampshire, and New York. But the drawing of arbitrary map lines had little effect on the yeoman farmers in the Upper Valley, who were clearing and planting with considerable hardship. Even in later years, their loyalties belonged more strongly to the towns on either side of the river than to the states.

As was true in other areas of the United States, the settlement of the Upper Valley was in part a land grab. Lines were drawn and grants were awarded which enabled certain privileged hands the right to establish townships and sell land. The most aggressive person to lay claim to the northern area west of the Connecticut River was New Hampshire's Governor Benning Wentworth, who in 1749 granted the township of Bennington in the farthest southwest corner of the disputed territory. Wentworth made a few other grants in following years, and then between 1760 and 1764 he issued some 150 townships west of the Connecticut, as well as some 50 more on the east side. Many of these townships lay directly along the river. In laying claim to the land west of the Connecticut, Wentworth's primary motivation was plain and simple greed. Each grant stipulated that a large plot — usually five hundred acres, but sometimes as large as eight hundred acres — be set aside for Wentworth himself. After making his many grants, Wentworth owned nearly one hundred thousand acres on paper.

After these grants were made settlement followed rapidly, and by the end of the 1760s much of the land on both sides of the Connecticut River was inhabited. Although townships had been issued in the name of New Hampshire, few settlers in the new territory felt allegiance to Wentworth's government. Portsmouth and the more inhabited parts of New Hampshire in the southwest were distant places for settlers in the Upper Valley, who rarely traveled farther than twenty or thirty miles from their farms.

Continued settlement in the Upper Valley did not draw Portsmouth nearer to the area. Overland transportation to the east was practically nonexistent, hindering the development of bonds with the established parts of New Hampshire. Since the Connecticut River was the primary transportation route, most early settlers in the Upper Valley came from the southern reaches of the river in Massachusetts and Connecticut, rather than from the settled regions of New Hampshire. Their common economic and religious backgrounds further reduced their ties to the provincial govern-

BENNING WENTWORTH. *Governor of New Hampshire,1741-1767. Oil on canvas, by Joseph Blackburn. Wentworth's tenure was the longest of any governor in British North America. Courtesy New Hampshire Historical Society.*

WESTERN REBELLION IN
NEW HAMPSHIRE & VERMONT

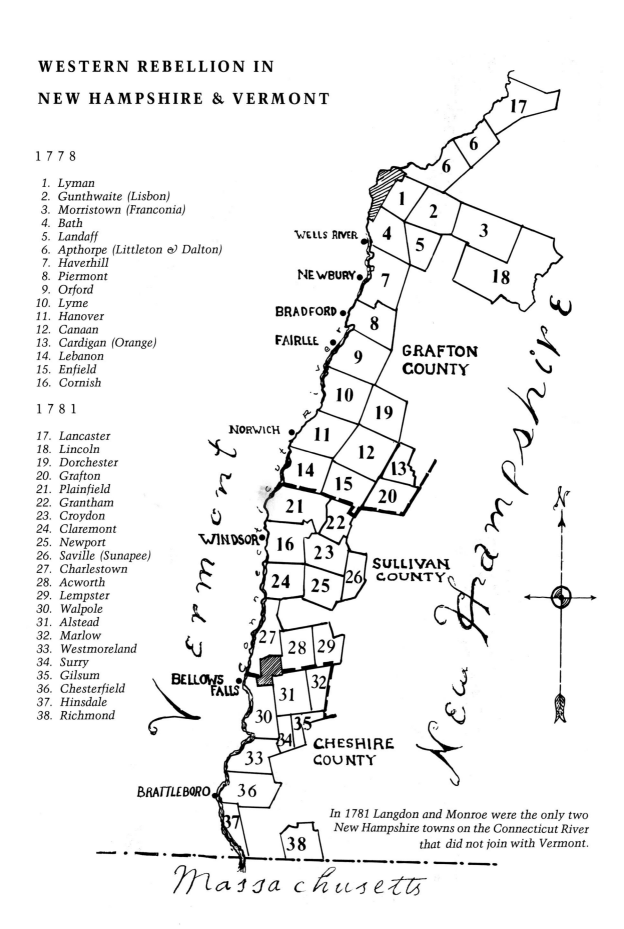

1778

1. Lyman
2. Gunthwaite (Lisbon)
3. Morristown (Franconia)
4. Bath
5. Landaff
6. Apthorpe (Littleton & Dalton)
7. Haverhill
8. Piermont
9. Orford
10. Lyme
11. Hanover
12. Canaan
13. Cardigan (Orange)
14. Lebanon
15. Enfield
16. Cornish

1781

17. Lancaster
18. Lincoln
19. Dorchester
20. Grafton
21. Plainfield
22. Grantham
23. Croydon
24. Claremont
25. Newport
26. Saville (Sunapee)
27. Charlestown
28. Acworth
29. Lempster
30. Walpole
31. Alstead
32. Marlow
33. Westmoreland
34. Surry
35. Gilsum
36. Chesterfield
37. Hinsdale
38. Richmond

WELLS RIVER

NEWBURY

BRADFORD

FAIRLEE

GRAFTON
COUNTY

NORWICH

WINDSOR

SULLIVAN
COUNTY

BELLOWS
FALLS

CHESHIRE
COUNTY

BRATTLEBORO

*In 1781 Langdon and Monroe were the only two
New Hampshire towns on the Connecticut River
that did not join with Vermont.*

Vermont

New Hampshire

N

Massachusetts

ment in Portsmouth. Geographically isolated, the settlers quickly developed a system of government in accordance with the prototypes they had known in Connecticut. This system was imbued with the idea of a strong, local government. Most settlers also believed that the popular branch of the legislature should be supreme in any constitutional government.

These political ideas of the early Upper Valley settlers did not conform to the realities of New Hampshire's royal government. Nevertheless, little friction existed between the western river towns and the Portsmouth government. Representation in the Provincial Assembly was only at the pleasure of the governor, and towns outside the original New Hampshire grant, with their more democratic leanings, were rarely invited to send delegates. In turn, the western towns paid little heed to official enactments of the assembly, but instead relied on loose and changing confederations among townships to defend against Indian attacks and to provide other measures of order.

The semiautonomous political and economic life of the Upper Valley ended with the collapse of the royal government in New Hampshire and the advent of the American Revolution. Yet the integration of the western towns along the Connecticut with the rest of New Hampshire was not easily accomplished. With the dissolution of the royal government, a long rebellion ensued. Problems had begun in 1774, when an extralegal legislature — the Provincial Congress — convened in Exeter to elect New Hampshire's delegates to the Continental Congress in Philadelphia. Royal Governor John Wentworth — nephew of Benning Wentworth — immediately denounced the Provincial Congress, but no heed was paid him. The Provincial Congress continued meeting in Exeter, and within a year it had a greater membership than the royal legislature. For one year New Hampshire had two legislatures — the legal, royal one located in Portsmouth and the extralegal one in Exeter. When Governor John Wentworth was forced to flee Portsmouth in July 1775, the royal government ceased to exist.

The Provincial Congress immediately assumed the status of a colonial legislature, filling the vacuum left by the collapse of the royal government. On the surface the transition made in governments occurred smoothly, presenting no difficulties. All New Hampshire towns appeared willing to transfer their allegiance from the royal government to the colonial one. But there were problems. Most importantly, the royal charter was no longer in effect, and the colonial government found it had no constitution or other document which defined its powers or the liberties of the people under its jurisdiction. Consequently, the Exeter government's foremost need was to prepare a document to establish the new government's legitimacy.

The drafting of New Hampshire's first constitution was a hasty affair. In October 1775 the colonial legislature asked for guidance from the Continental Congress "with respect to a method of our administering Justice and regulating our civil police. . . ." The Continental Congress responded in November, stating rather broadly that New Hampshire should "establish such a form of government . . . [which] will best produce the happiness of the people and most effectively secure peace and good order in the province." Receiving this advice, the colonial government formed a committee, which presented a constitution for acceptance on January 5, 1776. The legislature passed this constitution with no difficulties and subsequently called upon towns throughout New Hampshire to send representatives to the newly formed government. Now the trouble began.

Grafton County towns refused to accept the constitution or to send representatives to the new legislature. Much of their opposition lay in the fact that towns were not represented individually in the legislature. Being sparsely populated in comparison with the coastal part of New Hampshire, many of the Connecticut River towns were grouped together as units, each granted a single representative. This especially incensed the Grafton County towns, as it seemed to them that the royal government was not much different from the new one, "except that the Governor had the power in the former, and a number of persons in the latter." In neither case did towns in the Upper Valley feel they had any real representaton. To rectify the matter the Grafton County towns proposed "that every inhabited town have the liberty, if they please, of electing one member at least to make up the legislative body." This proposal corresponded to the Upper Valley inhabitants' belief that local town governments should have significant power.

At the center of the rebellion were the towns of Hanover and Lebanon, and it was Elisha Payne of Lebanon and Bezaleel Woodward and John Wheelock of Hanover who organized the growing protest. Officially, the rebellious group was called the United Committees. The "college party" was the more popular term, however, as several affiliated with Dartmouth College were influential in organizing the protest. Attempts were made by the Exeter government to mollify the Upper Valley towns, and in 1777 an offer was even made to convene a new constitutional convention. But it was too late. The rebellion had grown, and its focus had shifted. Leaders of the United Committees no longer saw their goal as one of political representation within New Hampshire; they now desired something much larger — the formation of a new political entity.

The rebellion continued to grow. In addition to their refusal to send representatives to the legislature in Exeter, the Upper Valley towns also withheld their tax quotas from the New Hampshire government. By 1777 the United Committees had been successful in detaching almost forty towns from the Exeter government, and its next move was to attempt a union between these towns and the towns on the western side of the Connecticut River. Such a union, it was hoped, would lead to the formation of a new state called New Connecticut. A further hope was that the capital of this state would be the new town of Dresden, created from the corner of Hanover where Dartmouth College is still located. This attempt to make Dartmouth College a political center became one of the primary goals of the rebellion.

The proposal to form the state of "New Connecticut" was immediately undercut. A second rebellion had developed in the territory west of the Connecticut River under the leadership of Ethan Allen, who sought independence from the claims of both New York and New Hampshire. His goal was to form a new state, "Vermont." Land speculation played a part in the rebellion's origin. Ethan Allen laid claim to over forty thousand acres of land — most of it located in the Champlain Valley — and his title was good only if New York claims were rendered invalid.

The Vermont rebellion overlapped with the Upper Valley one, since the new state Vermont would include half of the proposed New Connecticut. Undaunted, the rebellious New Hampshire towns made no attempt to thwart the Vermont rebellion. Instead, they sought to join it by becoming a part of Vermont. When the first Vermont legislature met in Windsor on March 12, 1778, a delegation was sent to propose that Vermont accept into its union sixteen New Hampshire towns, as well as other towns that might be desirous of such a union.

By joining Vermont, college party leaders realized that Vermont's population would be concentrated in the Upper Valley. They then planned to propose that Dresden be made capital of the new state. If this plan failed, then all of Vermont might be made a part of New Hampshire. Dresden — i.e., Dartmouth College — with its central location in such an enlarged New Hampshire, would serve ideally as the state capital.

Ethan Allen and other Bennington leaders of the Vermont rebellion had no desire to see their power usurped by the

Connecticut River towns, and they strongly opposed including New Hampshire towns in Vermont. Initially the Bennington party was outmaneuvered. Towns west of the Connecticut threatened to break from Vermont and form a new state with the towns across the river. To prevent such a move, sixteen New Hampshire towns — Lyman, Gunthwaite (Lisbon), Morristown (Franconia), Bath, Landaff, Apthorpe (Littleton and Dalton), Haverhill, Piermont, Orford, Lyme, Hanover, Canaan, Cardigan (Orange), Lebanon, Enfield, and Cornish — were admitted into Vermont on June 4, 1778.

Admission of these towns into Vermont solved nothing. Both rebellions continued throughout the Revolutionary War, as the Exeter government, the college party, and the leaders in Bennington struggled with each other for political power. In the end the college party lost. Shortly after the sixteen New Hampshire towns were admitted into Vermont, Ethan Allen and his brother Ira maneuvered to rescind their admission. In retaliation, the college party organized a campaign to bring the entire Upper Valley into Vermont. They almost succeeded when, in 1781, Vermont annexed thirty-eight New Hampshire towns despite the Allens' opposition.

This annexation, like the first, was short-lived, as the Continental Congress finally put an end to the continuing disputes and intrigues in the Upper Valley and Vermont. As a condition for acceptance as an independent state, Congress insisted that Vermont give up all claims to any territory east of the Connecticut

The Green Mountain Boys in council. From Vrest Orton,
PERSONAL OBSERVATIONS ON THE REPUBLIC OF VERMONT, *Rutland, Vt., 1981.*

River. Threats were also made, implying that if this condition were not met, New York and New Hampshire would be granted a common border along the ridge of the Green Mountains. In Bennington on February 23, 1782, the Vermont legislature voted to relinquish any claims east of the Connecticut River. To force the New Hampshire towns back into a union with the Exeter government, Congress also threatened in January 1782 to send troops to bring the rebellion to an end. This threat was sufficient to make most of the rebellious towns break with the college party.

Despite the many years of conflict, the rebellion in the Upper Valley ended remarkably peacefully and with little bitterness. But it did have some repercussions. In June 1784 a new state constitution went into effect, containing the provision that every town having 150 voters was entitled to one representative in the House, plus an additional representative for every 300 voters above that number. Towns with fewer than 150 voters were grouped together for representation. In part, the college party got what it originally wanted — representation for individual towns.

The new constitution also contained a provision that no "president, professor, or instructor of any college . . . shall at the same time have a seat in the senate or house of representatives, or council. . . ." This was the punishment meted out to Dartmouth College for having been so prominent in the Upper Valley rebellion. The provision stood until 1792, when a revision of the constitution struck out this clause.

With the conclusion of the Upper Valley rebellion, towns along the east side of the Connecticut River were for the first time fully integrated politically with the rest of New Hampshire. This process of integration has continued, and the antagonisms of two hundred years ago have largely been forgotten. The Upper Valley is now firmly divided between Vermont and New Hampshire.

2

Growth and Turmoil

THE 1790s TO THE 1830s

The Connecticut River

FOR YEARS the Connecticut River was the only cleared path into the forested Upper Valley wilderness. In the middle of winter early settlers used the river as a road, transporting their few belongings in wagons and sleds pulled over the ice and snow. When the water again flowed, other settlers paddled northward in log canoes. When the area was more settled, goods were shipped up and down the river. Overland roads were virtually nonexistent.

Flatboats originally carried most of the goods. They came into use shortly after English colonists established their first settlements on the Connecticut in 1633. Boatmen became so skillful with these craft that they were soon running them over the Enfield Rapids in Connecticut. As more settlements were established farther north, larger flatboats were built. These were run between the various falls, where the freight was unloaded, transported by teams, then loaded on flatboats again. Settlers near the falls often rented out their teams and wagons, profiting greatly by the need to transport cargo overland for short distances.

When the Upper Valley was settled almost 130 years later, flatboats were still the primary means of Connecticut River transportation. Most were quite large, built with a square mainsail in the middle of the craft, as well as a topsail. At times there was a third sail rigged above the topsail for use in very light winds. When the wind was unfavorable, the flatboats were propelled by poling. This was done with poles twelve to twenty feet long, made of white ash and with a socket spike in the lower end. A poleman placed the spike end firmly on the river bottom, then pressed the pole's upper end against his shoulder and walked from the front end of the boat to the mastboard. It was strenuous work, and progress was slow.

The transportation of goods by flatboats, unloaded and reloaded at every waterfall, continued until after the Revolutionary War, when the Upper Valley experienced a period of rapid growth. Both population and trade greatly increased, and there arose a demand for better transportation facilities. In retrospect, it seems apparent that the Connecticut River could not have remained the chief transportation route into the Upper Valley. In addition to its many falls, the river had other definite disadvantages. It was impassable by boat for four months during the winter. During the summer months it was also at times unnavigable when the water level was low. And no matter what was done to improve the river, transportation remained relatively slow.

Despite these facts, plans were made in the 1790s to increase the navigability of the Connecticut River. Proposed was a system of canals and locks around the principal falls. To facilitate the plans, the newly formed Vermont Legislature issued in 1791 a grant to establish "The Company for rendering the Connecticut River Navigable by Bellows Falls." A similar company, named "The Proprietors of the Locks and Canals on the Connecticut River," was chartered in Massachusetts in 1792. The first project undertaken by these companies was at South Hadley, Massachusetts. The route for a canal there was marked out in 1792. The canal was completed and opened in 1795, making the Connecticut one of the first rivers in the United States to be improved by canals.

The desire for more rapid transportation was connected with commercial rivalry between the river towns of Hartford and Springfield and the seaport towns of Massachusetts. As long as the Connecticut River remained the primary transportation route into the Upper Valley, Hartford and Springfield merchants could control much of the New Hampshire and Vermont trade. To insure continued control, these merchants sought to improve transportation on the Connecticut River. Such improvements, it was hoped, would permanently establish the river as the principal trade route to northern New England. But Boston and other Massachusetts merchants were interested in building canals and roads from the seaboard to the Upper Valley.

For several years those interested in the Connecticut River route were successful. A second canal with ten locks was opened in 1800 at Turner's Falls, near Deerfield, Massachusetts. In 1802 a third canal with eight locks opened at Bellows Falls. Two smaller upper canals — one at Sumner's Falls near Hartland, Vermont,

and the other at the White River Falls near Wilder, Vermont — opened in 1810 and completed the system. A sixth canal was built at Enfield, Connecticut, but this was not finished until 1829, and it contributed little.

With the opening of the first five canals, transportation of goods greatly increased on the Connecticut River. Newer and larger flatboats, called Durham boats, were built with a carrying capacity of sixteen tons and more. Often constructed of oak, they were sixty feet in length and eight feet in width. In the stern was a cabin for the crew. Iron, tools, millstones, salt, molasses, cloth, and rum were transported northward into the Upper Valley. In exchange for these goods, settlers sent south farm produce, potash, lumber, and maple sugar.

The time needed to complete the journey up and down the river greatly decreased. On the average it eventually

Connecticut River flatboat. From Lyman S. Hayes, "The Navigation of the Connecticut River," Proceedings of the Vermont Historical Society, 1916-1917. *Courtesy Vermont Historical Society.*

took just twenty days for the trip upriver from Hartford to Wells River, and ten days for the return trip downriver. The round trip between Hartford and Bellows Falls averaged two weeks, and the return trip from Bellows Falls usually took only three days — Northfield was reached the first day, Springfield the second, and Hartford the third.

The transportation business on the Connecticut grew and continued profitable for a considerable period. Until the 1820s the lower river communities controlled the best of the trade with Vermont and New Hampshire. Considerable competition was coming, however, from the eastern seaport towns. Merchants there had funded the building of the Middlesex Canal from Boston to the Merrimack River. This canal opened in 1803, and the following year the Fourth New Hampshire turnpike was completed to Grafton County. Two earlier turnpikes, called the Second and Third, had reached Claremont and Walpole in 1801 and 1803. Transportation from Boston to the Upper Valley, though expensive, was possible.

Largely in response to increasing competition from the seaboard towns, Hartford and Springfield merchants made a concerted effort in the 1820s to further improve river transportation. Their desire was to build an even more elaborate canal system. Among other ideas, it was proposed that a canal be built paralleling the Connecticut River from Northhampton, Massachusetts, to Barnet, Vermont. From Barnet a canal was to be built to Lake Memphremagog and possibly to Lake Champlain. Nothing came of these grandiose schemes. By now most New Hampshire businessmen preferred to invest in the development of turnpikes. There was also talk of railroads.

A final effort to keep the Connecticut River as the major transportation route came with the introduction of steamboats. It was hoped that these boats would reduce the time needed to travel up and down the river and thereby greatly decrease transportation costs. In the 1790s Samuel Morey of Orford actually launched a steamboat propelled by paddle wheels on the Connecticut, but it was

The steamboat BARNET. *From Henry W. Erving,* THE CONNECTICUT RIVER BANKING COMPANY, *Hartford, Ct., 1925.*

not until the 1820s that commerical attempts were made to navigate the river by steamboats.

The first attempt to travel the length of the Connecticut River by steamboat came in 1826, when the *Barnet* left Hartford, Connecticut. On the first day of the trip the boat failed to pass the Enfield Rapids and had to return to Hartford, where its machinery was strengthened. On its second attempt the *Barnet* passed the rapids, but when it reached Bellows Falls it again had to turn around, because it was too wide to pass through the locks.

To compensate for the narrowness of the locks and canals, six smaller steamboats were built. One of these, the *John Ledyard*, managed to travel farther north on the Connecticut than any other steamboat. In June 1831 the *Ledyard* left Hartford and journeyed northward past White River Falls. The boat continued up-river as far as Wells River, where just above the mouth of the Ammonoosuc it became stranded on a bar. Attempts were made to pull it over the bar to no avail. The *Ledyard* returned to Springfield, Massachusetts, and never traveled northward again.

The *Ledyard*, though small enough to pass through the river's locks, was not large enough to be economically viable. Both boats and locks needed to be larger if steamboat traffic was to be profitable. The Connecticut Valley Steamboat Company did operate steamboats on the lower reaches of the river, and for a while there were plans for running relays of steamboats between the various falls, unloading and reloading them as had been done with flatboats. But the days of canal and river transportation were ending. Roads were being improved, and by the late 1840s railroads were being built into the Upper Valley. After two hundred years the Connecticut River was ceasing to be a major transportation route.

NAMING THE RIVER

WHEN THE Dutch navigator Adriaen Block discovered the river, he named it De Versche Rivere — the "Freshwater River." This name was used by the Dutch for over thirty-five years, until they were forced by the English to abandon the river in 1650. English settlers never used the Dutch name. Instead, its name for them was always the Connecticut, taken from the Indian name Quinni-tuk-ut, meaning "long river." The "tuk" apparently signified a river whose waters are driven in waves by the tide or wind.

Although Connecticut was the name used by the English, there was little agreement as to its spelling. Governor Winthrop did use the spelling Connecticut seven times in his 1633 *History of New England*, but in the same book he also wrote Conecticot and Connecticott. William Bradford of the Plymouth Colony spelled the river's name at various times as Conightecute, Conightecut, Conightecutt, Coonightecutt, and Conightecute. Rogers Williams spelled it Quonihticut, Qunnihticut, and Qunnticut.

All told, more than forty spellings of the river's name were recorded in early histories, including Quinetucquet, Quenticutt, Quoncktacut, Canedicott, Canetticut, Connectecotte, Conectigus, Conittekock, Conitycot, Countticott, Conecticot, and Connite Cock. Why Connecticut came to be the preferred spelling is unknown. Perhaps it was simply that over the years this spelling seemed to conform most to the way people pronounced the name.

VIEW ALONG THE CONNECTICUT RIVER,
SHOWING WINDSOR, VERMONT, AND
MT. ASCUTNEY. *Gouache on paper, by
Nicolino Calyo, 1850. Below the town of
Windsor is the farm of S. E. Robbins, of the
the firm Robbins, Kendall & Lawrence. The
artist is depicted in the lower right, giving
instruction to "little Tommy Abbot." Note
how drastically cleared the land was then
compared to today. Courtesy Hirschl &
Adler Galleries, Inc.*

Logging on the Connecticut

GIANT WHITE pines were the first trees felled and transported down the upper reaches of the Connecticut River. In 1761 Jared Ingersoll of Connecticut received a contract from the British Navy to cut eighty "Mast Pines" along the river at any point between Deerfield, Massachusetts, and Haverhill, New Hampshire. The size of giant white pines reached 3 to even 7 feet in diameter and 120 feet in length. England was their destination, where they were to be used as masts for naval ships.

Bringing such massive trees out of the woods was a laborious task. Before a giant white pine was even felled, bushes and other obstructions had to be cleared and a bed prepared to cushion the fall of the tree. A wide path to the river was also cleared, made as straight as possible, since it was virtually impossible to turn a tree over a hundred feet in length. When a tree was cut, it was loaded onto a cart which, according to Robert Pike in *Tall Trees, Tough Men*, had wheels "eighteen feet high, to enable the big log, drawn up on chains beneath the axles, to clear obstructions." Forty or more oxen pulled the tree to the river.

Ingersoll's lumbering crew transported a total of 147 giant white pines to the Connecticut River, but 63 were declared "defective" — their insides were hollow. Two others broke when rolling down to the river, and a third was left behind. Driving the remaining 81 mast pines downstream was a perilous chore. The Connecticut, with its many rapids, falls, and bends, was a treacherous obstacle course for the drivers. One pine, three feet in diameter, broke on the Bellows Falls, and another was badly damaged passing the Deerfield rapids. Loaded on special cargo ships in Connecticut, the giant trees eventually reached England in 1764.

Even though abundant stands of giant white pine existed along the upper stretches of the Connecticut, the Upper Valley never became a major source for mast pines. Governors Benning and John Wentworth reserved the right for themselves to cut all giant pines in New Hampshire for the British crown. By selling the rights to cut these trees, they made a considerable profit. Unable to control the logging of mast pines in the remote and sparsely settled region of the Upper Valley, they stifled it by fining poachers. John Wentworth, for example, once traveled to the Upper Valley to confront loggers in the act of felling giant pines without permission. Because of these measures, Portsmouth remained New Hampshire's center for the mast trade.

Not all giant white pines were saved for masts. Pike notes that in 1769 a Windsor man named Dean was fined eight hundred pounds for having felled sixteen giant pines. Dean defended himself by arguing that he had only cleared a field to plant wheat, but records showed he had floated a half million feet of lumber down the river, selling it at a dollar per thousand. When Dean refused to disclose where he had hidden his money, he was jailed for four months. Other instances of illegal timbering occurred with regularity.

Lumbering was an early and common industry in the Upper Valley. Wood transported south could readily be sold to be made into boards, shingles, and staves, and in exchange the valley settler received finished goods. Early log drives on the Connecticut were common, though generally small. Most frequently logs were simply rolled into the river and driven uncontrolled to their destination, often far to the south in Massachusetts and Connecticut. The freely floating timber caused considerable damage along

Log sluice in Grafton, Vermont. Courtesy Vermont Historical Society.

Log drive passing under the Ledyard Bridge, about 1895. Looking east toward Hanover. The covered bridge between Hanover and Norwich stood until 1935. Courtesy the Montshire Museum of Science.

Log drive on an
unidentified river in
New Hampshire, about
1860. Courtesy the
Montshire Museum
of Science.

Log drive on the
Connecticut River. In
one bateau are an anvil
and brazier, used for
shoeing horses and
repairing tools. The
cook's raft and cabin,
called the Mary Ann, is
to the rear. Courtesy
Montshire Museum
of Science.

the way, striking against mills, bridges, and wharves. Much lumber was also wasted, as logs were always damaged by the uncontrolled drives.

The building of bridges and locks and canals on the Connecticut River brought an end to the early practice of uncontrolled drives. In order to prevent the destruction of these structures, the New Hampshire legislature passed a law in 1808 called "An Act Regulating the Mode of Putting Pine-timber into Connecticut River." The act spoke at length about the evils of the existing log drives, then stipulated that "all Pine Timber found floating in said Connecticut River [had to be] rafted, or under immediate care and controul [sic] of some person or persons. . . ." In accordance with this law, lumber was floated in rafts controlled by a small crew. Each raft was made up of "boxes" of logs sixty feet by twelve feet. At every falls the raft was broken into smaller boxes, and a toll was paid for each one passing through the locks. On the other side of the locks, the larger boxes were reassembled.

The rafting of logs down the Connecticut continued through the mid-nineteenth century. To make the journey more profitable, produce and heavy goods were frequently loaded on the rafts and transported downriver with the lumber. The trip was long and arduous. As many as eighteen rafts were floated together, with the men leading the drive living atop the logs. C. W. Bliss of West Fairlee, Vermont, recalled years later a rafting journey in May 1854, on which he did the cooking. "A rough board shanty nearly covered one box. . . . One end was used as dining-room and kitchen, the other for sleeping purposes. An old elevated-oven stove was used in cooking. In the sleeping end, a liberal quantity of straw was thrown loosely on the logs on which the men slept with their clothes. They lay in two rows with heads toward the sides of the raft and feet in the middle. I bought white bread at different points. I made brown bread, cooked potatoes, beans, tea and coffee. These constituted the whole bill of fare."

Passing through the locks with the rafts was especially difficult. Bliss recalled that in 1854 three days were spent breaking up eighteen boxes at Bellows Falls and reassembling them on the other side of the locks. "That day [a Sunday] I think there were at least five hundred people on the banks of the river and the canal watching the work. There was considerable competition between the men on the different rafts on the long stretch of still water above the dam to see which raft would get down to the canal first." The entire journey from north of Orford down to Middletown, Connecticut, lasted over a month.

Rafting continued as long as the Connecticut River served as a transportation route, ceasing only when the railroads displaced river traffic. Then, unhampered by locks or ships, the first major log drives in the Upper Valley began. Hundreds of thousands of logs were rolled every spring into the Ammonoosuc River, the Moose River, the White River, and other smaller rivers and streams, then floated down to the Connecticut. The rivers were swelled by melted snow, and the logs rushed downstream.

In 1868 twenty million feet of timber were cut in New Hampshire near the Canadian border, then driven down the river. It was the largest amount of lumber ever cut in New Hampshire, but in subsequent years large log drives on the Connecticut became commonplace. The two major drives were those of the International Paper Company and the Connecticut Valley Lumber Company. The International Paper Company's drives averaged seven million feet of lumber every spring. Driven down the Ammonoosuc, its thousands of logs were frequently held back from the Connecticut by a boom at Woodsville until the much larger drive of the Connecticut Valley Lumber Company passed. The International Paper Company's drive went only as far as Bellows Falls, where one of America's first pulp paper mills was established. No one wanted those logs floating in the river at Bellows Falls when the Connecticut

Valley Lumber Company drive came down from northern New Hampshire with twenty or thirty million feet of lumber.

The log drives down the Connecticut River were some of the longest in the world. The Connecticut flows a distance of 345 miles, and logs were driven from its origin at the Connecticut Lakes all the way down to Long Island Sound. It was a hazardous journey; many men lost their lives when they slipped and fell beneath the fast-moving logs. Obstacles were ever present. Logs jammed up behind bridges and islands, and numerous rapids and falls impeded the lumber. To the north was Fifteen-Mile Falls, said to be the worst place on the Connecticut to drive logs. To the south was Bellows Falls, which could take as long as three to six weeks to pass.

Log drives on the Connecticut continued into the twentieth century, coming finally to an end in 1915. That April the last drive began. More than five hundred men drove sixty-five million feet of lumber down from the Connecticut Lakes. Two men were killed along the way, and an ice jam at North Stratford, New Hampshire, backed up so many logs that houses and barns were flooded and railroad tracks were torn up. It was summer when the logs reached the Connecticut Valley Lumber Company mill at Mt. Tom, Massachusetts, concluding the decades of drives on the river.

THE LOCKS AT WHITE RIVER FALLS

IN 1808 MILLS OLCOTT, a Hanover lawyer and businessman, was active and successful in persuading the New Hampshire legislature to pass the law that said logs transported on the Connecticut River had to be "rafted" and under control. For Olcott, passage of this law was extremely important, as it meant that logs floating down the Connecticut would have to pay a toll at the locks he was building at White River Falls.

Because it was flooded with the building of Wilder Dam, the White River Falls (also called Olcott Falls) can no longer be seen. At this location in Lebanon, New Hampshire, just south of the Hanover line, the river fell thirty-seven feet in the course of a mile. Three rock bars made the falls particularly hazardous for navigation; their violence was famous.

The history of White River Falls improvements began earlier in 1806, when Gordon Whitmore persuaded Olcott to join him in building a slip around the falls to expedite the passage of lumber. The estimated cost was three hundred dollars. After two months' labor and an expenditure of five or six hundred dollars, it became apparent that more extensive work was necessary. Whitmore suggested building locks and canals around the bars on the east side of the falls. The estimated cost increased to four thousand dollars, and the project was expected to take two years.

Olcott agreed, but as Whitmore had no capital, he conveyed three-fourths of the property to Olcott and mortgaged the other fourth to him. Olcott was to provide all funds to complete the work, and Whitmore would supervise the operation. An upper dam was built in 1806, but an autumn freshet destroyed part of it. Quickly rebuilt, it was again damaged in the spring of 1807. For the third time Olcott paid to have it rebuilt.

By now it was increasingly apparent that the cost of building locks at the White River Falls would greatly exceed the estimated four thousand dollars. To obtain additional funds, Olcott brought his brother-in-law Ben Porter in as a new business partner. And then, to insure that his investments would pay off in the future, Olcott arranged two matters in advance of the completion of the locks.

The first was a charter granted by the New Hampshire legislature in June 1807, giving Olcott and his associates "the Privilege of Locking White River Falls." Included in the charter was a provision stipulating, "That said corporation for the space of twelve years next after the locks shall be completed, shall have full power to fix and determine the rate of toll to be taken by said corporation." Empowered to establish his own toll rates, Olcott set them higher than toll rates elsewhere on the Connecticut. Even after twelve years had passed, his rates remained the highest. The second matter was the law regulating the manner in which pine logs were placed in the river, assuring Olcott his toll for all lumber

transported down the Connecticut. He later remarked that this legislation made his venture profitable.

The locks and canals at White River Falls opened in the spring of 1810 and consisted of one dam at the middle bar followed by three locks, plus a second dam at the lower bar and two more locks. Each lock was seventy feet long and fourteen and one-half feet wide. The walls were stone without mortar, and the gates were worked by a windlass and chain without balance beams.

The costs far exceeded the estimated four thousand dollars, climbing to over twenty-three thousand dollars. Nevertheless, the locks and canals proved profitable to Olcott. In 1811 he bought Ben Porter's interest, making Olcott the sole proprietor, and for the next thirty-seven years, until his death in March 1848, he operated the locks at a profit.

The Olcott or White River Falls, as seen from the Vermont side in 1882, near the present site of Wilder Dam. Courtesy Baker Library.

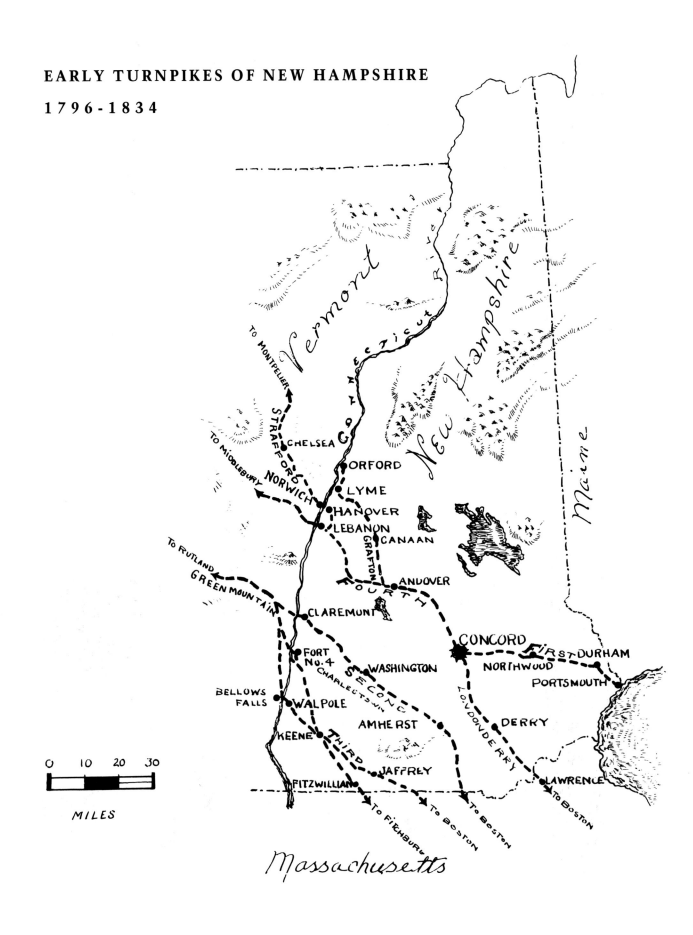

EARLY TURNPIKES OF NEW HAMPSHIRE

1796-1834

MILES

0 10 20 30

New Hampshire Turnpikes in the Upper Valley

CUTTING roads through the virgin forest of New Hampshire was an arduous task, and consequently most early settlements were made along navigable rivers. Only after settlements had existed for a few years were the first roads built, and these were not meant to replace the rivers as transportation routes. Instead, most early roads connected various settlements within towns, or, occasionally, one or two towns with each other. The Haverhill town records, for example, show that it was voted in March 1764 "to lay and clear a road from the lower end of Haverhill to the Upper Meadows this summer." Other town records tell of similar road construction in and around the separate townships.

Because the first settlements were along rivers, so were the first roads. Construction was easier there. Roads built from river to river, passing through unbroken forests, were more difficult. When completed, forest roads were usually so crude that only riders on horseback or in heavy oxcarts could pass over them.

The first major road leading to the Upper Valley was one which roughly paralleled the Connecticut River on its east side. Referred to today as the Dartmouth College Highway, it was originally called the Great Road. It followed an earlier Indian trail. Prior to the 1750s a road had been cut up the valley as far as Fort No. 4, and in 1752 a proposal was made to extend that road as far north as the Coos Meadows (Haverhill). Continuing hostilities with the Indians and French made the construction of such a road impossible, however, and only a horse track led northward from Charlestown into the Upper Valley. When the Upper Valley was first settled in the early 1760s, many settlers chose to travel this path rather than to make the journey on the river. Following little more than blazed trees, they made their way northward with pack horses.

In 1768 or 1769 this path was widened and improved, making it passable for wagons. In early August 1770 Eleazar Wheelock traveled this road when he moved to Hanover to found Dartmouth College. The Great Road served both sides of the Connecticut River until 1790, when a river road on the Vermont side was built. The Great Road, however, continued to bear the most traffic, competing with the river for trade until the completion of the railroad along the Connecticut in 1849.

Sometime after 1787 an attempt was made to improve overland travel from the Upper Valley toward the southeast. A road was partially constructed from Hanover to Boscawen via Moose Mountain, North Enfield, and Canaan. Intended as a major route to Concord, the road provided little improvement in travel. The road trip from Hanover to Boston still took approximately six days.

The first overland routes of significance from the Upper Valley to other parts of the state were the post roads. In February 1791 the New Hampshire legislature established four post routes, two of which looped between Concord and the Upper Valley. The post roads were marked through the forests by blazed trees, and at best were rough bridle paths. All transportation over them was either on foot or on horseback. The purpose of the post roads was not to transport goods, but rather to hasten communication between towns and communities. In the wake of the Upper Valley rebellion this was especially important. With improved communication, the post roads helped integrate the Upper Valley into the daily political and business affairs of the state. However, the major trade route for the area was still to Springfield and Hartford along the Connecticut River and the Great Road.

Toward the end of the eighteenth century a demand for improved inland roads was heard throughout the United States. As the states had not been granted the right to raise taxes for internal improvements, such as roads, legislatures chartered privately owned and operated turnpikes or toll roads. The nation's first such toll road completed was the Lancaster Turnpike, running sixty miles from Philadelphia to Lancaster, Pennsylvania. It opened in 1792.

Continued growth in the Upper Valley and in other parts of New Hampshire and Vermont resulted in a similar demand there for improved overland transportation routes. Roads from the Upper Valley to Concord and Boston were considered especially important. Following the idea of the Lancaster Turnpike, the New Hampshire legislature chartered in June 1796 a company called the "Proprietors of the New Hampshire Turnpike Road." The road built by this company, commonly called the First New Hampshire Turnpike, ran from Concord to the Piscataqua Bridge in Durham. After the construction of this road, a "turnpike craze" rapidly developed in New Hampshire, and by 1810 close to fifty turnpike companies had been incorporated. Among the most important were those chartered to meet the demands of the expanding Upper Valley.

A coach stopping at an inn in the snow. From Barrows Mussey, OLD NEW ENGLAND, *New York, 1946.*

The Second, Third and Fourth New Hampshire turnpikes all ran to the Upper Valley. Completed in 1801, 1803, and 1804, they ran from Amherst (N.H.) to Claremont, New Ipswich to Walpole, and from Concord to Lebanon-Hanover. The three looked like an extension of spokes, emanating from the hub of Boston. The intention was to divert trade from the Connecticut River and to make Boston the Upper Valley's commercial center.

In addition to these turnpikes, two others were important for the Upper Valley. In 1804 construction began on a turnpike four rods (66 feet) wide, running from Orford Bridge on the Connecticut through Orford, Lyme, Canaan, Grafton, and Danbury to meet the Fourth New Hampshire Turnpike in Andover. Called the Grafton Turnpike, this road opened in 1806. A third turnpike into Grafton County was chartered in 1804. Called the Croyden Turnpike, it ran southerly through Lebanon, Enfield, Grantham, Croyden, and Newport to the Second New Hampshire Turnpike in Lempster. It followed essentially the same route as Route 10 does today. The Croyden Turnpike had less significance for the area, because it did not provide a direct route to Concord.

Among these turnpikes, the Fourth New Hampshire Turnpike was perhaps the most important. In 1805 an advertisement appeared in the *Dartmouth Gazette* that "a line of stages is erected to run from Hanover to Boston." The route was along the Fourth New Hampshire Turnpike. Passengers spent two nights on the road, at Concord and Nashua. The fare was $6.90. By 1807 stages were leaving Hanover and Boston every Monday and Friday at 5:00 A.M., arriving in Concord as early as 5:00 P.M. Here passengers were exchanged, and the stages then returned to Hanover and Boston on the second day. By 1809 the Concord-Hanover stage was running three times a week.

Although popular, early travel over the turnpikes was rough. In 1792 Jeremy Belknap described in his *History of New Hampshire* the nature of road building:

"The manner of making a new road, through the wilderness, is this: First, a surveyor and his party, with the compass and chain, explore the country, and where they find the country suitable for a road, the trees are spotted, by cutting out a piece of bark, and at the end of every mile the number is marked on the nearest tree. Then follow the axe-men, who clear away the bushes and fell the trees, in a space of three rods [49½ feet] wide, cutting them as near as possible to the ground, that the stumps may not impede the traveling. . . . Rocks are either turned out of the road, or split by gunpowder, or heated by fire and then softened by water."

This extensive labor, according to Belknap, did not produce a finished road. He continued: "Roads are not brought to perfection at once, especially in rocky and hilly land; but after the first operations they are passable for single horses and teams of oxen. As the earth is opened to the sun, many wet places are dried, and brooks are contracted; and as the land is more and more cleared, smaller streams disappear." Belknap also noted that: "for crossing small streams, the beaver dams are found very safe and convenient. They are three or four feet wide at the top, which is level with the water above, and is always firm and solid."

Roads had improved by the turn of the nineteenth century, but still they were rough. Stones had not been removed, and construction through marshy areas consisted of laying logs across the roadway and filling in the chinks with dirt — so-called corduroy roads. Until as late as 1816, wagons had neither iron axles nor springs. The noise made by the wagons rattling over the roads was extremely loud and was called "homespun thunder." At times a coach became stuck in the mud or a rut. At other times the grade of a hill would be too steep for the horses to negotiate with a full load. When this happened, it was expected that the passengers would step out of the coach and push.

In the 1820s travel over the turnpikes improved with the introduction of new coaches. In 1827 Louis Downing, a carriage maker in Concord, made the first Concord coach. Called "the perfection of the stagecoach," it had "a strong, heavy body, carried on great leather straps called thoroughbraces, a stout top capable of carrying a number of passengers, and a boot for the carriage of mails and luggage." The Concord coach was considered so convenient and comfortable that the first railroads converted Concord coaches to carry passengers by rail.

TAKE NOTICE !!!!

WE the subscribers, at Henry Clough's Tavern, in Enfield, (N. H.) having of late, in company with a number of respectable ladies, without provocation, been *treated* and *insulted* in an unbecoming manner, do hereby warn and advise all those, who may have occasion to journey by or near said inn, to regard it as the residence of beings, who merit the derision of mankind.

N. R. SMITH,
BENJ. WALES,
DAVID THOMSON.

Hanover, July 29, 1805.

DARTMOUTH GAZETTE, *August 2, 1805.*

To meet the needs of coach travelers, many farmers along the turnpikes converted their homes into taverns or inns. Located about every two or three miles along the road, the larger ones served the coach trade and the more affluent travelers. These were usually two-story frame houses. Below was the public room, with a large, open fireplace and sanded floor. Within the public room was a bar supplied with rum, gin, brandy, cider, flip (a hot, sweet and spiced cider or beer), and toddy. Above were the sleeping rooms. These were never heated, and warming pans were used to take the chill from the beds. Washing facilities were in a public washroom.

Traffic over the turnpikes was at its height from the 1820s through the 1840s. The roads were used by a great many people, especially in the early winter when farmers transported their marketable goods to Boston, Newburyport, and Salem. Yet, despite the increase in traffic, the turnpikes did not fully replace the Connecticut River as the major transportation route to the Upper Valley at this time.

In the 1820s pressures began to mount in the towns to make the turnpikes free roads. Over the years portions of the roads were made free, and then they swarmed with more traffic than ever. But only for a short time. Everything changed practically overnight in 1847, when the first railroad reached the Upper Valley. As one observer noted: "The thoroughfare with its . . . whirring stagecoaches teeming with life and animation, became almost as silent as a graveyard. The taverns which dotted every mile were silent, too, and the great stables at the stage taverns and elsewhere, filled with emptiness, looked like monuments of another period."

After almost fifty years of use, the turnpikes to the Upper Valley became virtually abandoned. In Grafton County the "College Branch" of the Fourth New Hampshire Turnpike, leading from Lebanon into Hanover, served only local needs for the rest of the nineteenth century. Not until well into the twentieth century was the old turnpike rehabilitated for the use of automobiles.

The Enoch Hale Toll Bridge was the first bridge over the Connecticut, built in 1785 at Bellows Falls. On the east side stood a large hotel, later called the Tucker Mansion. The bridge was 360 feet in length and 60 feet above water. Stage coaches made stops on the bridge to allow passengers a view of the falls below. Oil on canvas, by Frederick J. Blake, about 1792. Courtesy Rockingham Free Public Library.

BRIDGES OVER THE CONNECTICUT

BUILT IN 1785, the bridge at Bellows Falls, Vermont, was the first to span the Connecticut River. Eleven years later, three other bridges were completed over the river — at Springfield, Massachusetts, between Cornish and Windsor, and between Hanover and Norwich.

Although the lower part of the Connecticut was settled by English colonists in the 1630s, no bridges were built over it for 150 years. Ferries, usually large flat boats pulled with ropes or chains, were used for crossing. Ferries were also used by the first settlers in the Upper Valley. In April 1763, for example, the proprietors of Hartford, Vermont, voted to run a ferry across the river to Lebanon. A large boat, capable of carrying men, horses, and carts, was built. During the winter months the ferries did not operate. People simply drove their wagons across the ice toll free. The building of bridges over the Connecticut was connected with the construction of turnpikes and roads. Most

Rates of Toll Established by Law July 1st, 1804.			
	Cents		Cents
Foot Passengers		Three horse do do	20
Horse & Rider	6	Four horse or Oxen	25
One horse Chaise or Sulkey	12½	One horse Sled or Sleigh	10
One horse Coverd Carriage	12½	Two horse do do	15
Two horse do do	25	Four horse do do	20
Four horse Carriage	25	Each additional horse	3
Mail Stages	25	Neat Cattle & mules	2
One horse Waggon or Cart	10	Horses	4
Two horse do do	16	Sheep Hogs & Calves	½

bridges were placed at locations complimentary to proposed turnpike routes. Replacing ferries, the bridges became part of an expanding overland transportation network linking inland settlements.

The first bridges over the Connecticut were toll bridges. Rates for passage varied, but generally they were similar to ferry rates. In 1804 the toll at the Bellows Falls bridge was three cents "for each passenger on foot." A rider on a horse paid six cents, and "each four wheel carriage with two horses," twenty-five. A "loaded sleigh or sled with two horses or oxen" was fifteen cents, as was a "pleasure sleigh with two horses." And a "cart or wagon with two oxen or horses" was a penny more. Sheep, hogs, calves, and goats were ten cents "the score or half cent each."

Built of wood and uncovered, these first bridges rotted relatively quickly. The Hanover-Norwich bridge, for example, collapsed in 1804, barely eight years after its construction. A second bridge, built in 1805, was also open and required extensive repairs within two years. Because of

The Tucker Toll Bridge. In 1840 the frame of the Enoch Hale Bridge was discovered to be decayed. A covered bridge was built fifteen feet higher and directly over the old one. The old bridge was then cut away and allowed to fall into the water. The Tucker Toll Bridge was made toll free in 1904 and stood until 1931. Courtesy Rockingham Free Public Library.

weather damage, covered bridges were introduced to protect the wooden trusses, and by the 1820s few uncovered bridges remained.

The number of bridges over the Connecticut River increased as the river declined in importance as a transportation route. By the 1830s, when turnpike travel was reaching its height, bridges connecting the roads had become a necessity. Railroads virtually eliminated the river and turnpike traffic in the late 1840s, but not the need for bridges over the Connecticut. Railroad bridges spanned the river as soon as rails were laid to the water's edge.

The Orford Ridge Houses

IN THE YEARS after the Revolutionary War and well into the 1800s the Upper Valley was a thriving region. Town populations rapidly increased, and village centers developed around saw mills, grist mills, general stores, and other small shops. The crude houses of the earlier years were replaced by more finished wooden structures. Sometimes the houses were even built of brick.

Just how prosperous this era was is often forgotten today. In the case of Orford, New Hampshire, for example, travelers who see the row of seven Federal-style houses perched on a ridge overlooking the Connecticut River are at a loss to explain how they came to be built there. Where did the original owners amass the money to build such elegant houses in so small a village?

The first house on Orford Ridge, built by Obadiah Noble in 1773. Courtesy Alice Doan Hodgson.

A croquet party at the Roger's house on Orford Ridge, August 1868. Although no longer owned by the Rogers' family, the house remained largely unaltered at the time of the photograph. Courtesy Alice Doan Hodgson.

The answer to that invariable question is usually sought in something outside Orford and the Upper Valley. Over the years it has been suggested that the seven houses were built by wealthy sea captains who chose to retire in Orford. Another explanation is that wealthy lumbermen built their residences here. Another version has it that wealthy sheep farmers built the houses. Others have insisted that wealthy summer residents were the original owners.

None of these explanations is accurate. The answer is rather simple and straightforward, as has been detailed by Alice Doan Hodgson in her book *Orford, New Hampshire: A Most Beautiful Village*. Each house was built by an Orford resident between 1773 and 1839, a period when Orford was a growing and flourishing town. And each house was built with money earned within the community.

The town of Orford was chartered in September 1761, although the first family did not arrive until October 1765. For the next sixty-five years the town experienced steady growth, reaching in 1830 a peak population of 1,829 — about triple the present population. The town was a prosperous farming community, with several grist and saw mills and other small mills. The first settlement in Orford was not on what locals came to call the Ridge, but rather along the Connecticut River. The first house on the Ridge was built in 1773, eight years after the first Orford family's arrival. It was built by the town's first minister, Obadiah Noble, who, after living two years on a low plain near the river, decided to move to higher elevation safe from flooding.

The site on which Noble chose to build was in the middle of the Ridge. Here he built Orford's first two-story house, a structure with one large room and one small room on both the ground and second floors. For over thirty years this was the only house on the Ridge. Noble lived in this house for only four years, leaving Orford in 1777. Subsequently the house was sold to William Simpson, who converted the house to an inn. In 1799 the house was sold again, this time to Samuel Morey. In addition to the house in the middle of the Ridge, Morey also purchased the land where the other six Ridge houses were eventually built.

Within a year Morey began to make additions and improvements to the two-story house, bringing it to its present state in 1804. The beginning of the Ridge houses as they are today thus starts with Morey. His stands in the middle, and on either side three other houses were built. Much of Morey's money was earned from sawmill and lumbering operations, but he is better known locally as the inventor of the first steamboat powered with a paddle wheel. In 1793 he launched on the Connecticut River a log dugout with a steam-powered paddle wheel at the prow. Over the next few years, Morey made improvements to this first steamboat, including the use of side paddle wheels in 1797. Side paddle wheels made steamboat travel possible, but Morey was unable to obtain sufficient financial backing to make his invention commercially successful. That honor went to Robert Fulton.

Morey was well known for several other inventions. He heated and lighted his house with water gas, prepared by mixing heated carbon, steam, oxygen, and vapor of turpentine. In 1826 he took out a patent for a gas-powered internal combustion engine. This engine operated on principles similar to those of present-day automobile engines. To prove his engine could propel a carriage, he attached one to a wagon in his workshop. The engine worked so well that the wagon crashed into a wall.

In 1814 Morey sold two plots of land at the southern end of the Ridge. The southernmost plot was purchased by John B. Wheeler, an Orford merchant who operated an inn and tavern in town. Wheeler completed his house in 1816 from architectural plans attributed to Asher Benjamin. In 1816 Wheeler traveled to attend his son's graduation from Dartmouth. While there he learned of attempts to turn Dartmouth into a state university, and subsequently he gave the college faction one thousand dollars. This money was used to obtain the services of Daniel Webster, who successfully helped defeat a legal effort to revoke the college's charter. Dartmouth's Wheeler Hall was named in his honor.

The house north of Wheeler's was built by John Rogers, a young Orford lawyer. Begun in 1817, the house was completed four years later. Its facade was copied from Wheeler's. Rogers worked as a lawyer until 1830, when he retired to a farm near Indian Pond. Later he moved to a farm near Lyme, where he successfully occupied himself as a sheep farmer until his death in 1859.

The house between the Rogers and Morey houses was built at three different periods. In 1805 Morey built for his parents a one and one-half story structure, which now stands at the rear of the present house. Both his parents had died, when Morey's daughter Almira married Leonard Wilcox in 1819. As a wedding present, Morey had a two-story addition built to the first structure, and this house he presented to his daughter and son-in-law.

Wilcox was a successful lawyer in Orford. Eventually he became a judge for the New Hampshire Superior Court. He also served a term as United States senator, having been elected in 1842 to serve the unexpired time of Franklin Pierce. Almira did not live to share Wilcox's successes. She died in 1830, shortly after giving birth to her sixth child. Three years later Wilcox remarried, and in preparation for this marriage he added in 1832 a one-story front.

The fifth house on the Ridge was built by Dyar T. Hinckley, an Orford merchant. In 1822 Hinckley purchased land north of Morey's house, and two years later he erected a two-story brick house, now painted yellow. It was the first brick house in Orford. The house is particularly known for its circular stairway, which ascends from the front hall. Hinckley did not live long in the house, as he died in 1834 at age forty-two.

The sixth house built on the Ridge was also made of brick. Its owner, William Howard, was a manufacturer of beaver hats. Howard came to Orford in 1799, when he was twenty-four years old. Before moving to Orford he had served an apprenticeship as a hatter in Norwich, Connecticut. Upon his arrival in Orford he began manufacturing beaver hats. The quality of his hats was said to be the finest, and he apparently prospered. In 1825, when Howard was fifty years old, he purchased the northernmost piece of land on the Ridge and began building his house. Construction continued for four years, and when completed, the house rivaled the Wheeler mansion in size and elegance. Within this large house lived Howard, his second wife, and twelve children — seven from the first marriage and five from the second.

The seventh and last house to be built on the Ridge belonged to Stedman

Willard, another merchant. Willard came to Orford from Massachusetts in 1813 at the age of fifteen. In Orford he found a job as clerk in the store of the merchant Wheeler. In 1824 Willard married Wheeler's daughter Meriel, having opened a business with another partner a year earlier. Six years later Willard entered a partnership with his father-in-law, which continued until Meriel's death in 1837, one month after the birth of her seventh child.

After Meriel's death a peculiar rivalry appears to have developed between Willard and Wheeler. In 1838 Willard purchased the land between the Morey and Hinckley houses, and then, after marrying again, he began in 1839 to build a house on the site. His house was very spacious, and some said he was determined to build a bigger and better house than that of his former father-in-law Wheeler. In this he never succeeded, as Wheeler's property was always assessed higher.

Those were the original owners of the seven Ridge houses in Orford. Over the years the houses were rented out or sold at different times. When, in the latter half of the nineteenth century, Orford began to experience a severe decline in population, many of the Ridge houses began to suffer a decline in appearance. By the beginning of the twentieth century the Howard house was sadly neglected, and Morey's house had been changed drastically. Today Orford is no longer the community it was when the Ridge houses were built. Nevertheless, all seven Ridge houses, with the Howard and Morey houses restored, retain their elegance; five are still used as year-round residences.

The Orford Ridge houses, viewed from the south, about 1900. From right to left are the Wheeler, Rogers, Wilcox, Morey, Willard, and Hinckley houses. The Howard house cannot be seen. Courtesy Alice Doan Hodgson.

Nathan Smith, Founder of the Dartmouth Medical School

MEDICINE was something most early settlers tended to by themselves with an assortment of home remedies. Wild indigo was used to treat typhoid, and St. Johnswort was applied to wounds. A tea made of the dried flowers of bee balm was said to be good for fever, and milkweed and butter-and-eggs were both made into skin lotions. Other plants and herbs were used for a variety of medicinal purposes.

The use of these home remedies, however, did little to prevent the outbreak of different illnesses, and as the population increased, so did the incidence of disease. Particularly deadly in the area were repeated outbreaks of dysentery. In Lyme, New Hampshire, five adults and twenty-five children died in the months of August and September 1800. A year later, dysentery killed seven children in Lyme within seven days.

In the latter part of the eighteenth century, advances began to be made in medicine. Innoculation against smallpox was introduced, and in 1771 Lebanon established a "pest house" in a remote corner of the township where people could receive innoculations. Another advance was the widespread introduction of patent medicines — some useful, some not — at the beginning of the nineteenth century. Quackery still existed, however, and a number of doctors were more known for their eccentricities than for their expertise. Dr. Joseph Lewis of Norwich, Vermont, acquired a reputation for his dirty buckskin suit which he refused to clean or replace. Lewis became even more well-known when he obtained the corpse of an elderly black named Cato and boiled it behind his house. His purpose

was to obtain a skeleton — something scarce in an age when cadavers were hard to come by legally.

Although there were eccentrics and even quacks in the area's early medical profession, there were also several genuine pioneers in the field of medicine. The Hanover doctor Dixi Crosby excelled at surgery when he practiced in the mid-1800s. Lyman Spalding, born in Cornish, founded in 1820 the *United States Pharmacopoeia*, a compendium of drugs and medicinal substances commonly used in pharmacy and medicine. But the most famous physician from the Upper Valley was undoubtedly Nathan Smith. Smith pioneered major advances in the field of surgery, and in 1797 he founded the medical school at Dartmouth College. He also contributed to the founding of the medical schools at Yale University (1813), Bowdoin College (1821), and the University of Vermont (1822).

Despite Smith's later eminence, it was almost by chance that he became a doctor. In 1783 a farmer in Chester, Vermont, suffered a compound fracture of the leg while lumbering. The treatment at the time for such an injury was amputation, and Josiah Goodhue — a celebrated surgeon in the Upper Valley — was called from nearby Putney to perform the operation. The event created considerable excitement in the village of Chester, and many of the more curious gathered in the house of the farmer to witness the amputation. As the operation began, Goodhue asked for a volunteer to hold the injured limb. A young schoolmaster stepped forward from the group, supported the leg, and "even ligated the arteries as

NATHAN SMITH. *Oil on canvas, by Ulysses Dow Tenney. Courtesy the Hood Museum of Art.*

they were clamped, and did so without tremor."

The schoolmaster's name was Nathan Smith. When the operation was completed, Smith impulsively asked Goodhue for an apprenticeship in medicine. Goodhue agreed, but advised Smith first to spend a year of schooling with Reverend Samuel Whiting in near-

Entry from Nathan Smith's ledger, July-September 1810. Courtesy Baker Library.

by Rockingham, Vermont. That advice was followed, and thus began the medical education of one of the most important figures in American medicine.

Nathan Smith was born in 1762 in the town of Rehoboth, Massachusetts. While he was still a child, his family moved to Chester, Vermont — very much a frontier region then. Life generally con-

sisted of farming, hunting, and fishing, and little was provided in the way of formal education. Probably Smith was taught by his parents; there is no record that he ever attended any of the small village schools. Sometime after the Revolutionary War he assumed the position of Chester's village schoolmaster. Little else is known of Smith's life before that impulsive moment in 1783 which marked the beginning of his medical career.

After the year with Reverend Whiting, Smith served a three year apprenticeship with Goodhue at Putney. Then, at age twenty-five, Smith moved to Cornish, New Hampshire, and — without a medical degree — opened a medical practice. After two years of practice in Cornish, Smith concluded that his training was inadequate. With the encouragement of Goodhue, he applied to Harvard Medical College. When accepted, he closed his office and sold his house to finance his instruction in Cambridge. Smith attended Harvard Medical College (founded 1782) from 1789 to 1790. He was the fifth student to graduate from the College, and among its early graduates, he became the most famous. Upon graduation he again returned to Cornish, where he reopened his practice.

At the time Smith began his work as a doctor, the medical profession was dominated by the theory that all disease had a humoral or nervous origin. Benjamin Rush was the major proponent of this idea in the United States, and common treatments recommended by him included bleeding, sweating, and purging. Surgery was, in comparison, very limited and usually performed only in emergencies. It consisted generally of reducing fractures and performing amputations. There was frequent call for such procedures. Accidents were common in the country, where injuries occurred while cutting timber, milling logs, and raising houses. Other common injuries were related to horses and teams or to being run over by wagons.

After the Revolutionary War there was an increasing interest in surgery, and

Smith became one of the leading and most innovative surgeons in America. In the early 1800s he devised a surgical procedure for the treatment of osteomyelitis. This is a disease which often resulted from typhoid fever and led to a bone infection. In more severe cases, the only known treatment was amputation of the infected limb. Smith's method was to puncture the infected bone and to extract the dead part. Over the years Smith performed the operation numerous times, saving many limbs. Smith was so far in advance of the medical and surgical knowledge of his time that this procedure was not generally known until after 1874. And only after World War I did it become standard treatment throughout the world.

In addition to developing his treatment for osteomylitis, Smith was the second person in America to operate to remove an ovarian tumor. His initial operation was performed in Norwich, Vermont, on July 5, 1821. (Ephraim McDowell had performed the first such operation eight years earlier in Danville, Kentucky.) Smith was the first in the United States to perform the operation of staphylorrhaphy for cleft palate. He operated widely on cataracts; he introduced a new method for fashioning the skin flaps in amputation of the thigh; and he contributed innovative ideas for the treatment of arm and leg fractures. His surgical and medical genius alone would have given Smith an established place in medical history. However, he was also instrumental in the founding of four New England medical colleges.

Having first practiced after a customary apprenticeship of three years, Smith was well aware of the inadequacies in New England medical training. Determined to make improvements, he applied in August 1796 to the trustees of Dartmouth for a "Chair of the Theory and Practice of Medicine." At the time the college had been in existence for only twenty-five years. The trustees favored the idea, but because of a lack of funds they voted to postpone the decision for one year.

The trustees also hesitated because the other three medical schools then in existence in the country — Harvard, the University of Pennsylvania, and the Medical School of King's College (later Columbia) — were located in large cities. Unlike Dartmouth, their parent institutions were also well established. The creation of a medical school by a fledgling institution in a rural part of the country carried with it definite risks.

Undaunted, Smith decided to enhance his prestige in the eyes of the trustees through a period of study in Edinburgh and London — cities at the time considered world capitals of medical erudition. Borrowing money from friends, Smith spent eight months in study abroad. Shortly after his return to America, he began on November 22, 1797, to hold medical lectures at Dartmouth — still without final approval from the trustees. He delivered a full ten-week course of lectures before returning to Cornish, but it was not until August 22 of the following year that the Board of Trustees took the final steps to establish the Dartmouth Medical School.

For thirteen years Smith managed the school almost singlehandedly. Lyman Spalding, an apprentice, at times taught chemistry; Alexander Ramsay gave the anatomical lectures in 1808; and a Dr. Noyes, who practiced locally, frequently lectured when Smith was called out of town on a case. Although Smith was essentially its only teacher, the school flourished immediately. In 1807 thirty-five students were enrolled. That same year President John Wheelock was reportedly so stimulated by one of Smith's lectures that he opened evening prayers in the chapel with these words: "Oh Lord, we thank Thee for the oxygen gas, we thank Thee for the hydrogen gas, and all the gases. We thank Thee for the cerebrum, we thank Thee for the cerebellum, and for the medulla oblongata."

By 1812 student enrollment at Dartmouth Medical School stood at seventy-seven. Dartmouth soon graduated more medical students than Harvard — due in

The Old Dartmouth Medical School building, about 1855. The building was completed in 1811 and stood until 1963. The observatory still stands. Courtesy Baker Library.

part to less stringent admission requirements, in part to lower costs for the school, and in large measure to Smith's own presence.

Because of his reputation, Yale turned to him to help establish a medical school in New Haven. Initially, Yale's president opposed Smith's appointment, as Smith had "expressed doubts as to the truth of Divine Revelation." Nevertheless, Yale's trustees chose Smith, and in October 1813 he began lectures in New Haven. As at Dartmouth, student enrollment steadily increased at Yale after Smith's arrival. It was also at Yale that Smith completed some of his most important work, including a treatise on typhoid fever. In this paper he challenged the accepted methods of purging, sweating, and bleeding to reduce fever, and instead advocated a cold water and milk treatment. Little was added to this treatment of typhoid fever until the advent of antibiotics in the 1940s.

In 1821 Smith helped found yet another medical school at Bowdoin College in the newly formed state of Maine. For the next four years Smith traveled every spring from New Haven to Brunswick to teach, gradually delegating one subject after another to personally trained successors. By 1823 forty-nine students were enrolled at Bowdoin Medical School. Six years later the school graduated more doctors than any other medical school in all of New England.

While performing his duties at Yale and Bowdoin, Smith also began to travel in the summer of 1822 to Burlington, Vermont, where he lectured and helped organize faculty for a fourth medical school. Smith continued these diverse activities until he suddenly became ill in July, 1828. He never fully recovered, and for the last six months of his life he was able to work only intermittently. He died on January 26, 1829.

IT IS NOT known for certain, but it appears that one person cured by Nathan Smith's innovative surgery may have been Joseph Smith, founder of the Mormon Chuch. Joseph Smith's family lived in Lebanon, New Hampshire, when in the winter of 1812-1813 an epidemic of typhoid fever spread through the Upper Valley. The epidemic was extremely severe, and several towns with populations no larger than one thousand lost as many as fifty persons within eight or twelve weeks.

All the children in Joseph Smith's family contracted the disease that winter, but all recovered except the seven-year-old Joseph. His typhoid fever led to osteomylitis — a bone infection which causes long segments of the bony shaft to die. Standard treatment was the application of poultices and plasters to the inflamed flesh, usually with little effect. Inevitably, the dead bone separated and lay in the center of an abcess cavity, draining continuously. Amputation of the infected limb usually followed.

Joseph Smith's left leg swelled and after two weeks a surgeon was called. He incised the leg from knee to ankle to allow for drainage. When the leg still did not heal, a second incision was made down to the bone. The bone was not perforated, however, and Joseph Smith's condition worsened. Other surgeons were consulted and amputation by Dr. Nathan Smith was recommended.

Joseph Smith refused to assent to amputation, and Nathan Smith consequently obtained permission to carry out an experimental operation. No anesthetics were used; the young boy was simply restrained by his father. Holes were bored into the bone, and the affected parts were broken off. Shortly after the operation, Joseph Smith began to improve. Recovery was slow, and for three years he walked on crutches. During his adult life he continued to walk with a limp. Nevertheless, Joseph Smith was extraordinarily fortunate to live near the Dartmouth Medical School, for in 1813 Nathan Smith was probably the only person in the country who could have saved his leg.

JOSEPH SMITH, *founder of the Mormon Church. Courtesy Vermont Historical Society.*

Dartmouth and the Dartmouth College Case

EDUCATION was a matter for frequent disagreement during the early years in the Upper Valley. In fact, education was at the center of one of the area's longest disputes. Neither curriculum nor any other specifics of learning was at issue. Instead, the concern was over who rightfully controlled Dartmouth College. When the case was finally settled, not only had Daniel Webster enhanced his reputation as a lawyer, but a legal precedent had been set with far reaching consequences for American business.

Called the Dartmouth College Case, the dispute originated in a conflict between John Wheelock, then president of Dartmouth College, and the college board of trustees. Wheelock had been appointed president in 1779 by his father Eleazar Wheelock, the school's founder. Both father and son appear to have viewed the college presidency as a legacy, to be handed down to a family member. In accordance with this attitude, John Wheelock's tenure as president was generally autocratic.

As Richard Morin recounts in his article "Will to Resist, The Dartmouth College Case," Wheelock faced no opposition for the first twenty-five years of his reign, even though he often defined the college's needs in terms of his own personal interests. The situation changed, however, when several new trustees were appointed in the first part of the 1800s. Unwilling to accept passively all presidential acts, the majority of these trustees soon entered into open disagreement with Wheelock. The rift between President Wheelock and the trustees widened, and in 1811 the trustees declared in a seven-to-three vote that college authority did not rest in the president alone, but in a majority of the executive officers, of whom the president was only one. The trustees continued to curtail Wheelock's power, and in November 1814 they even voted that he be "excused from hearing the recitations of the Senior Class. . . ."

Seeing his powers curtailed, Wheelock decided to fight back by enlisting the support of the public and the New Hampshire legislature. To this end he presented the trustees with a resolution, calling upon the Legislature "to examine . . . into the situation and circumstances of the College . . . to enable them to rectify anything amiss. . . ." The trustees voted down Wheelock's resolution. Not to be put off, Wheelock next wrote an eighty-page pamphlet, attacking at length the trustees and their unwillingness to allow the State to examine them. The pamphlet (coauthored by Reverend Elijah Parish, a close friend of Wheelock's) was published anonomously and widely distributed. It achieved its desired effect. Public outcry against the trustees was so great that in June 1815 the state legislature passed a bill establishing a committee "to investigate the concerns of Dartmouth College . . . and the acts and proceedings of the Trustees . . . and to report a statement of facts at the next Legislature."

The state-appointed committee made an inquiry into Dartmouth's affairs in the late summer of 1815, essentially concluding that nothing was amiss. The committee's report did not receive widespread circulation, however, and remained filed away for eight months. In response to Wheelock's actions and the subsequent inquiry, the Dartmouth

JOHN WHEELOCK. *Oil on canvas, by Ulysses Dow Tenney. Courtesy the Hood Museum of Art.*

trustees met in August 1815 and voted eight to two to remove Wheelock as president of the college. In his place was appointed Reverend Francis Brown from North Yarmouth, Maine.

The trustees hoped that the dismissal of Wheelock would put an end to the matter, but just the opposite occurred. Wheelock's dismissal led to increased public support for him, especially within certain influential circles. Some also saw this as an opportunity to punish Dartmouth for its leadership in the Upper Valley rebellion. Consequently, in June 1816 the New Hampshire legislature claimed a right for the state "to amend and improve acts of incorporation of this nature" — i.e., corporation charters which were "hostile to the spirit and genius of a free government," as Dartmouth's charter was labeled by the legislature.

Acting upon this claimed right, the legislature subsequently passed a bill, which among other things changed the name of Dartmouth College to Dartmouth University. It likewise increased the number of trustees from twelve to twenty-one. The legislature furthermore created a "Board of Overseers" which had the power to "confirm, or disapprove . . . votes and proceedings of the Board of Trustees." In this manner Dartmouth was transformed from a privately controlled institution into a state-controlled one.

On August 26, 1816, trustees of both the college and the newly constituted university convened separate meetings in Hanover. Because of a lack of a quorum, the trustees of the university had to adjourn, leaving the college board in control of the institution. The college trustees promptly adopted a resolution declaring that they did "not accept the provisions of an act of the Legislature of New Hampshire approved June 27." A moment of burlesque then followed. The governor discovered he was not empowered to call for a new meeting of the university trustees. New legislation had to be passed, and it was not until February 1817 that the university trustees first met.

When they did meet, they voted to reorganize Dartmouth College as Dartmouth University and to dismiss Brown as president, appointing John Wheelock in his place. Wheelock seemingly had achieved what he wanted, but Dartmouth College refused to disappear. The college trustees continued to meet, and Brown was retained as president. The college trustees also filed suit, challenging the constitutionality of the legislature's actions.

The result of these many actions and counteractions was that for the next two years there were two different institutions in Hanover — Dartmouth College and Dartmouth University. Each claimed that it alone had a legitimate right to exist. In terms of buildings, the newly formed Dartmouth University appeared the victor. Officials for the university quickly occupied Dartmouth Hall — which also contained the library — and the adjoining chapel building. But in terms of students and faculty, Dartmouth College was the winner. Most of the faculty remained loyal, and almost all the students chose to continue in the college. To carry on instruction, a large hall was rented for use as a chapel and classrooms.

Ironically, the man who initiated the action leading to the establishment of Dartmouth University did not live to see the results of his actions. In the spring of 1817 John Wheelock died, just months after his appointment as president of the newly organized university. His death changed nothing, as what had been set in motion continued. Both the university and the college held classes in Hanover.

In the struggle to demonstrate legitimacy, there were frequent clashes. In August 1817, for example, both the college and the university elected to hold their commencements in the meeting house on the customary date prescribed by the college bylaws. Hearing rumors of a threatened seizure of the meeting house by university members, sixty college students armed themselves with clubs and canes and occupied the building. When university students appeared, they were turned away by guards at every

DANIEL WEBSTER. *Oil on canvas, by Chester Harding, 1828. Courtesy the Hood Museum of Art.*

*Mary Marshall Dyer,
from her book,* THE RISE
AND PROGRESS OF THE
SERPENT FROM THE GARDEN
OF EDEN TO THE PRESENT DAY:
WITH A DISCLOSURE OF
SHAKERISM, *Concord, N.H., 1847.*

Mary Marshall Dyer and the Enfield Shakers

WOMEN'S RIGHTS in the United States were minimal through most of the nineteenth century. The right to vote was denied to women, and when they married they automatically lost the right to own property or to start a lawsuit. If for any reason a woman and her husband separated, she also had no legal right to keep her children.

This absence of legal rights placed a considerable burden on women, as Mary Marshall Dyer discovered when her husband Joseph joined the Shaker community in Enfield, New Hampshire. Unwilling to follow him in his newly found religious convictions, she was confronted with the loss of both her economic well-being and her children.

Founded in the latter part of the eighteenth century by "Mother" Ann Lee, the Shakers believed in celibacy and in the communal ownership of all property. To practice their beliefs, they established various communities. One of the earliest was located in Enfield, New Hampshire, on the south side of Lake Mascoma. Founded in 1782, the community lasted until 1923. The Shakers were known for their simplicity and industriousness, and, despite rumors of lewd practices which often followed them, there existed little friction between Shakers and non-Shakers. There were moments, however, when the two worlds came into conflict, and one such moment occurred when Mary Marshall Dyer left the Shaker Village in Enfield.

Mary Marshall was born in Northumberland, Coos County, New Hampshire, on August 7, 1780. According to her own account, she "possessed a poor state of health" from age seven to sixteen. "My ill health was my only trouble," she wrote. Little else about her childhood was included in her recollections, and nothing more is known. In 1799, at age nineteen, Mary Marshall married Joseph Dyer of Canterbury, Connecticut, and that same year they settled in Stratford, New Hampshire. The following year she gave birth

A partial view of the Enfield Shaker community, looking north over Lake Mascoma, about 1877. Courtesy Baker Library.

Enfield Shaker women, about 1898. The dress and manner of the Shaker women had changed little since Mary Dyer began her long campaign against the Enfield community in 1817. Courtesy Baker Library.

to her first child, a son named Caleb. A daughter, Betsey, was born in 1802, and a second son, Orville, in 1804. After the birth of their third child, the couple had an opportunity to exchange their farm for one in Stewartstown, New Hampshire, near Canada. Here a third son, Jerub, was born in 1806. In 1808 this farm was sold, and a new one was purchased in the same vicinity. Her last child, Joseph, was born there in 1809.

Mary and Joseph Dyer were prosperous as farmers. According to her account, they had a two hundred-acre farm "with a good stock of cattle, and had besides four hundred acres of land in the centre of town, intended for farms for our sons." There were few difficulties in these first years of marriage, Mary wrote, except for her husband's drinking. On the whole, however, she characterized him as "one of the best of husbands; and I verily believe he would still have treated me kindly if it had not been for the Shakers." Joseph vigorously denied his wife's charges that he was often drunk. He was also less kind in his portrayal of her character during the years they lived together. According to him, Mary was not only a bad mother and an adultress, but she was given to fits and temper tantrums. Whether his or Mary's account was true or only exaggeration is impossible to say.

In 1811 both Mary and Joseph Dyer traveled to Enfield to visit the Shaker community. The visit apparently made a favorable impression on Joseph, but not on Mary. What exactly ensued after this first visit is unclear. Mary wrote in one of her accounts, "The more I saw of the Shakers, the worse I felt." She also stated that her husband was an accomplice in a scheme to remove her children to the Enfield community.

Joseph, contradicting Mary, swore that she had willingly joined the Shakers. "Even after this time [the first meeting with the Shakers in 1811], Mary professed to be fully established in faith with the people called Shakers, until she left them in January, 1815. . . ."

There is likewise complete disagreement between the two as to the circumstances which led to their joining the Shakers. Almost the only point agreed upon is the fact that in 1813 — almost two years after their first meeting with the Shakers — they decided to enter the community at Enfield. Joseph accordingly sold their farm and property, and the entire family began to live with the Shakers. Two years later, in 1815, Mary left. According to her, she "escaped"; according to Joseph, she "absconded."

If Mary and Joseph Dyer had been a childless couple, there might have been no further dispute between them. Or if they had continued their fight, no doubt it would have remained a private dispute in which the general public had little interest. The issue of children, however, and who possessed the right to their custody, had wide implications for American society. Mary and Joseph Dyer's private dispute became a public affair.

A decision to join the Shakers was never a light one. Becoming a Shaker was far more than the acceptance of a set of religious tenets or beliefs. It meant the adoption of a particular and definite way of life. This way of life, determined by the Shaker elders, was defined by numerous exact rules. For example, work tasks were assigned. The women performed most household chores, including the making of clothing, while the men did most of the farming, made furniture, and worked as blacksmiths. This division of labor was established in part to insure the separation of the sexes during working hours. Other rules, dictating separate dwelling wings, dining tables, and even separate doorways, maintained an almost continuous separation of men and women. Rules governed other aspects of daily life, and many were meant to thwart the expression of individuality. Shaker craftsmen were not allowed the use of carvings or ornamental moldings which might express personal feelings. Bedframes were to be painted green, and a craftsman was never to leave an identifying mark on his work. Rules governed the most minute points of personal behavior, including table manners. The rules even went so far as to forbid playing with cats and dogs. In every possible area of daily living, Shakers were expected to obey their elders without question.

Essential to the Shaker way of life was a vow of celibacy on the part of its members. To insure that this vow was kept, men and women were physically separated, and husbands, wives, and children who joined were usually further separated by being placed in different "families." These separations were meant to eliminate prior attachments and to insure that personal feelings did not interfere with the Shaker love for all humanity.

A wife had much to lose if her husband chose to join the Shakers against her wishes and she did not agree to join. But even if she followed unwillingly, she still found herself separated from husband and children. For men, the situation never posed a problem. An unbelieving husband had to give his consent before his wife was allowed to leave him and join the Shakers.

How many cases existed similar to Mary and Joseph Dyer's is uncertain. A few came to light in various states, but none aroused public sympathy. To a large extent public concern was lacking because the women were in no position to defend themselves or to make their cases known. Shakerism generally appealed to poor and uneducated rural people, with the result that the wives most likely to be placed in Mary Dyer's situation were also the least able to take any action.

Not willing to lose her children, Mary Dyer sought help from the state legislature. In 1817 she spoke before the New Hampshire House, making a strong impression with harsh and lurid descriptions of Shaker practices. A committee was appointed to consider a bill that would make joining the Shakers legal grounds for divorce. No action was ever taken by the New Hampshire legislature, however, and Mary's appeal went unheeded.

Failure to obtain legislation did not stop Mary's attacks on the Shakers. Most of the rest of her life was devoted to excoriating them and her husband. For the next fifty years, she wrote numerous pamphlets and books which purported to be exposés of Shaker depravity. In her writings she presented affidavits from former Shakers, testifying that the founder of Shakerism, Mother Ann, was

everything from a fortune teller to a sadist to a prostitute. She then peddled these publications throughout New England. Joseph Dyer, in turn, periodically published material meant to discredit her.

Mary Dyer's scathing attacks were read avidly by a great many, but they had little effect. In fact, the venomous tone of her writings made her appear shrill and hysterical — a charge still echoed today. The ferocity of her attacks might in part be explained by her personality. She was considered a willful person, and one state legislator recalled, ''Her tongue is an unruly member, with a world of iniquity in it, if you cross her.'' But personality is only part of the explanation. Knowing she had no legal rights to her children, she most certainly realized that the legislature would act in her favor only if convinced her children had been placed in a depraved and ungodly situation.

In the end Mary Dyer was unsuccessful. Her exaggerations compelled many to lose sight of her real and legitimate concern — a woman's right to her children and a part of the family property. Too often the repeated attacks only clouded the issue and inspired a debate whether the Shakers really were as she claimed. Despite the public's skepticism Mary Dyer persisted, always insisting that the central point was: ''When a man having family joins the Shakers, he should also forfeit his right of guardianship, relative to his property; or at least relative to so much of it as might in the judgment of the civil authorities, be adequate for the comfortable maintenance of his wife, and such part of his family as are not of age to act for themselves, thereby they shall not be compelled to join the Shakers.'' Only after Mary Dyer's death in 1867 did women gain the rights she demanded.

RELIGIOUS SECTS IN THE UPPER VALLEY

THE HILL country of the Upper Valley and other parts of Vermont were especially fertile areas for new religions, such as Shakerism. No doubt the isolated existence of many settlers contributed to this, as did the economic upheavals and uncertainties which emerged when traditional farming ways began a rapid decline. A profusion of religious revivals and the conflicting demands of differing religions most certainly also played a part.

The most famous person from the Upper Valley to establish a new religion was Joseph Smith, founder of the Mormons. Born in Sharon, Vermont, his family migrated westward to New York in 1816, when Smith was eleven years old. Although only a young boy when he left, the years spent in the Upper Valley had profound influences on him and his family. In particular, the harsh and isolated years in Sharon influenced the family's belief in God as a personal friend with whom you had conversations.

Another person from the Upper Valley who founded a new religion was John Humphrey Noyes. Born in 1811 in Brattleboro, Noyes preached that Christ had reappeared, making possible a life of perfection on this earth. Noyes later added to his teachings the doctrine of "complex marriages," which allowed for open sexual relations among members of his community as long as "male continence" or *coitus reservatus* was practiced to prevent the conception of children. When the townspeople of Putney learned of this practice, they forced Noyes and his followers to flee to Oneida, New York, in 1847.

Other lesser figures also roamed the countryside. In 1817 Isaac Bullard, wearing nothing but a bearskin girdle, gathered a group of "pilgrims" in Woodstock, Vermont, and led them across the mountains into New York. Bullard, a champion of free love, considered washing a sin and boasted that he had not changed his clothes in seven years.

At times the end of the world was said to be nigh. William Miller, a reformed atheist, preached throughout New Hampshire and Vermont that the Apocalypse would arrive in March 1843. One hundred and forty thousand souls would be saved, Miller said, and he invited the faithful to assemble on hilltops and in the church belfries to be nearer to God when the day of reckoning came. When nothing happened, Miller proclaimed the end would come in March 1844. This second failure of the world to end dashed Miller's standing as a prophet.

John Humphrey Noyes, about 1851. From George Noyes, RELIGIOUS EXPERIENCE OF JOHN HUMPHREY NOYES, *New York, 1923.*

The Noyes Academy in Canaan

IN 1835 THE newly opened Noyes Academy in Canaan, New Hampshire, became embroiled in a bitter dispute. The reason: the academy was one of the first schools in the United States to make an active effort to educate blacks beyond the grammar school level.

When an academy was first planned in Canaan, there was no thought of educating blacks. Like other New England

Alexander Crummell. After leaving Canaan, he studied theology in Boston and Cambridge, England, then served as a missionary for twenty years in Liberia, West Africa. In 1873 he returned to Washington D. C., where he was rector at St. Luke's Church until 1894. From Alexander Crummell, THE GREATNESS OF CHRIST, *1892.*

schools, the academy was intended for white males. One thousand dollars was raised by Canaan citizens in the early part of 1834, and a half acre of land was purchased to build a schoolhouse. Chief among the contributors was Samuel Noyes, and the school was named for him. Application was then made to the legislature for a charter, which was granted July 4, 1834. The charter provided for the "education of youth."

On the same day that the charter was granted several of the contributors declared that the Noyes Academy should be established "upon the principles of the Declaration of Independence," and that pupils should be admitted "without distinction of color." The reasons for this declaration lay in the antislavery agitation then prevalent in the United States. Riots had broken out in New York City in 1834, then spread to New Jersey, as the antislavery agitation reached its height. The call to open Noyes Academy to black youths was intended as a show of support for the Abolitionists and their agitation.

On August 15, 1834, the proprietors of Noyes Academy met to decide whether they would indeed allow blacks to attend their school. After a lengthy meeting, thirty-six of the fifty-one proprietors present voted to admit blacks. Those opposed, having lost this vote, quickly called for a town meeting to be held on September 3. At this meeting a resolution was passed, stating, "We view with abhorence every attempt to introduce among us a black population, and we will use all lawful means to counteract such introduction." No friends of the school took part in this meeting, and the resolution passed with eighty-six affirmative votes.

The vote at the town meeting did not represent a majority, as over three hundred names were entered on the Canaan voter check list. Because only a minority of the town's citizens had voted for the resolution, George Kimball, a principal proponent of the academy, concluded that a majority favored the admission of black pupils. He consequently went ahead with plans to open the school, and within a month the first classes began. By January 1835 thirteen black youths had traveled to Canaan to attend the school.

Few documents exist which recall those first months when the Noyes Academy opened. One letter remains, however, written by Alexander Crummell some sixty years after the events in Canaan. In May 1835, Crummell — then a sixteen-year-old black youth — traveled from New York to Canaan with three other boys near his age. His letter, written in 1897, recounts his arrival and the last few months Noyes Academy remained in existence.

The journey to Canaan was arduous, he wrote: "Our journey thither was tiresome and painful. On the steamboat, from New York to Providence, we were driven to the deck and thus exposed, bedless and foodless, to the cold and storm of the Sound. All the way from Providence to Boston, from Boston to Concord, from Concord to Canaan, a journey of some 200 miles, we were refused inside passage and driven to the top of the coaches. Not a hotel would serve us meals; nor could we get shelter at night."

In contrast, he was greeted with great friendliness upon his arrival in Canaan. In the same letter he wrote: "We arrived in Canaan in May and found some twelve other colored youth and one young woman. Nothing could be more cordial than our reception at Canaan." He continued: "It was the first step, in our lives, into the world of freedom, brotherhood and enlightenment." According to Crummell's letter, the early summer weeks of 1835 revealed no signs of discord. "At once we began our work, entering upon the study of the classics and mathematics; and our delight and satisfaction seemed unbounded . . . altho the people

of the village were unaccustomed to pupils of our race, we saw nowhere any signs of dislike."

By July, however, "signs of dislike" were very evident. Rumors began to circulate in Canaan that the village was to be overrun with Negroes from the South, that slaves were coming to line the streets with their shanties and to inundate the town with paupers and vagabonds. On July 4, 1835, a band of approximately seventy men, all armed with clubs and other such weapons, assembled in the town and marched to the Noyes Academy. Their intention was to tear down the building. As they approached, a window in the second story was suddenly thrown open and Dr. Timothy Tilton, a town magistrate, appeared. He issued a warning, and then in a loud voice began to note down the names of the men present. Fearful that they would be held accountable for an unlawful act, the men quickly dispersed.

Although many of the seventy men present that day were from Canaan, the majority were not. In fact, a major portion of the opposition to Noyes Academy originated outside of Canaan. In Concord, New Hampshire, the political center of the state, a great many opposed the academy. The surface reasons for their opposition lay in the belief that a Negro school in New Hampshire would serve to embitter the South and would consequently lead to a dissolution of the Union. This opposition led to violent agitation throughout Grafton County.

The mob meeting on July 4 was followed by another, which formed one week later on July 11. According to one witness: "They met at the old church in large numbers as before. William Campbell was moderator; they were noisy and excited, more so, if possible, than on the previous occasion. The only point I could gather in their proceedings was that the 'nigger' was a nuisance, and must be removed from town." Exhortations to destroy the school building were again raised at this second meeting, but none of the men present could be roused to perform a lawless act. Consequently it was resolved to hold a "legal" town meeting on July 31 to see "what measures the town will take to expel the blacks from the town of Canaan."

The Canaan town hall was crowded with men on July 31, and the meeting that followed was memorable for its disorder as well as for the many resolutions passed that day. By now those who favored the Noyes Academy had been intimidated into silence, and there was no opposition to those who had decided to destroy the schoolhouse. William Allen Wallace, in *The History of Canaan, New Hampshire*, noted that among the resolutions passed at this meeting were:

"Resolved that we consider the Colored School in this town a Public Nuisance and that it is the duty of the town to take immediate measures to remove said nuisance."

"Voted the town take immediate measures to remove the house in which the colored school is kept."

"Voted that the measures adopted by the town for removing said building, be commenced by the 10th day of August at 7 A.M. and be continued from day to day, without intermission, so as to satisfy the calls of nature, until the moving of said building be completed."

After this "legal" town meeting the mob believed it could lawfully do what had been unlawful before. Early in the

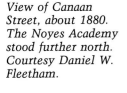

View of Canaan Street, about 1880. The Noyes Academy stood further north. Courtesy Daniel W. Fleetham.

morning on August 10, a large band of men again formed in Canaan and began to march towards Noyes Academy. Passages from letters, quoted in Wallace's history recall some of what happened:

"I was sitting at my desk writing. Saw a man, Mr. B., pass with an iron bar. Soon I saw several more pass with bars and axes. Now a wagon loaded with chains hurries along. I looked out at the door. The street was full of people and cattle in all directions." The intention was to drag the building off its foundation with the help of oxen. Another letter recalled: "The team is attached. Ninety-five yoke of cattle. It is straightened. The chains break. They try again and again the chains break! Almost in vain do they try. Thermometer ranges at 116 in the sun. At half past 7 P.M. they had succeeded in drawing it into the road, when they adjourned till next day."

That night the chains needed to be mended, but no blacksmith in Canaan would mend them. The chains had to be taken elsewhere. As before, many of the men in the mob came from Enfield, Dorchester, and Hanover. Apparently the oxen used to drag the building were also from surrounding communities.

The following day the destruction of the Noyes Academy continued. An eye-

witness recalled in a letter: "Tuesday, the 11th, the progress of destruction was more rapid. The chains held firm when the order was given to 'straighten the team.' A little before noon they had reached our store where they halted in front, and at once demanded that a barrel of rum should be rolled out or they would demolish the doors." And in the same letter: "These men persisted in their crime, until they hauled the house on to the corner of the Common, in front and close by the old church. They arrived on the spot just at dark, so completely fagged out, both oxen and men, that it was utterly impossible to do anything further. There it stands, shattered, mutilated, inwardly beyond reparation almost."

Less than a year after it had opened, the Noyes Academy in Canaan was destroyed. The black youths who had attended it were likewise gone, having left shortly after the events on August 10 and 11. They left by wagon, and as they departed a mob assembled once again and fired a field piece in the direction of the wagon as it passed. The Academy building was later moved to another location, and attempts were made by the town to repair it and reopen it for the education of white youths. At one time a teacher was hired and a few pupils attended, but after six or eight weeks the school was discontinued. Other attempts to open it also failed. Then on the night of March 7, 1839, someone set fire to the building. No efforts were made to save it.

THE UNDERGROUND RAILROAD

ALMOST everyone in the Upper Valley has heard at some time of the "underground railroad" which operated in the area. Tales of runaway slaves being aided in their escape are without doubt the most familiar aspect of black history in the region. Yet, despite general familiarity with the subject, few specifics are ever recounted. Lyme, Hanover, Hartland, and Windsor are known as stopping points where slaves were hidden until they could safely continue their journey northward. A few houses in these towns are thought to have served as hiding places.

Unfortunately, the lack of certainty about details will probably continue. In the years before the Civil War, when blacks were aided in their flight from the South, those involved in the illegal activities of the underground railroad left but a handful of written documents about their work. After the Civil War most historians were not interested in this important part of Afro-American history,

with the result that few accounts were gathered from those who had participated in it. Consequently, the history of the underground railroad in Vermont and New Hampshire remains unclear and somewhat mysterious.

One person who did reconstruct the history of the region's underground railroad was Wilbur H. Siebert. In his book, *Vermont's Anti-Slavery and Underground Railroad Record*, Siebert recounted the efforts made in Vermont to aid runaway blacks. Based on firsthand accounts and stories he collected, it is the only book to examine extensively this subject in Vermont's history.

Of course, the underground railroad was not a railroad at all. It was a network of those opposed to slavery, who were willing to take considerable risk to aid blacks in their escape from the South. Hiding a runaway slave was illegal, and often a fugitive slave was pursued by an armed slave hunter. According to Siebert, the Vermont underground network first started in the early 1820's and continued into the first years of the Civil War. The system was quite extensive, and fugitive slaves entered into Vermont at five different points — via the Connecticut and Battenkill Rivers, near Bennington, a few miles south of Lunenberg, and at Lyme, New Hampshire.

Via the Connecticut to Brattleboro was an important entry point for slaves traveling from Connecticut and Massachusetts. From Brattleboro many slaves traveled toward Townsend, through Chester, Woodstock, and eventually to Montpelier. This was apparently the most traveled route along the underground railroad in Vermont. Other fugitives chose to follow the Connecticut River northward. There are, however, no known stations along the Connecticut until Windsor. Whether some runaways who left Brattleboro simply followed the river, making friends along the way until they reached Windsor, is not known.

In Windsor, a house that once stood on State Street across from the prison is said to have been a hiding spot for runaways. From Windsor a slave traveled five miles north to Hartland, where "Lame" John Smith sheltered fugitives in the parsonage beside the Methodist Church. A short distance from Hartland, in Hartland Four Corners, lived Edmond Barrett, who helped slaves toward Woodstock. Others leaving Hartland journeyed twelve miles

to Norwich, where Stephen Carver Boardman hid many in a cellar in his cornfield.

One of the few surviving accounts of the underground railroad in Vermont recalls how Boardman once hid a slave, his wife, and his four-year-old child in the cellar, first wetting their feet with spirits of camphor to throw pursuing bloodhounds off the scent. When a slave hunter arrived with three bloodhounds, a U.S marshall, and deputies, Boardman refused permission to search his grounds as the posse had no warrant. After an exchange of angry words, the group left to obtain a warrant. Near sundown Boardman led the slave family from the cellar to a back road, where he told them to wait.

At nightfall, Boardman reappeared along the road with a wagon and drove the three fugitives twenty-five miles to the Central Vermont Railroad — probably the Randolph station. Here they were put on the morning freight train in care of a crew member who had performed the same service on several previous occasions. They remained on the train until Montpelier, or possibly even Burlington.

Montpelier was apparently the largest center in Vermont for the underground railroad, but unfortunately nothing is recorded about the number of fugitive slaves who passed through the state capitol. It is another unknown in the uncertain history of the region's underground railroad.

3

Agrarian and Industrial Transformation

THE 1830s TO THE 1880s

The Transformation of Farming: From Self-Sufficiency to Sheep

IN THE YEAR 1830 the town of Orford had a population of 1,829. Ten years later its population had declined to 1,707. Orford's decrease in population during that decade was not an aberration. It marked the beginning of a long downward trend which continued through the nineteenth century and into the twentieth. By 1850 Orford's population had declined further to 1,406, and by 1890 only 916 people lived in the town.

Many other towns in the Upper Valley registered similar population declines, some as early as 1810. The downward spiral continued in subsequent years, spreading to more and more towns. By 1830 the overwhelming majority of towns in the Upper Valley and other parts of Vermont and New Hampshire had begun long and steady declines.

The most important contributing factors involved agriculture. The first severe blow was manmade, coming in 1808 when President Jefferson imposed an embargo on the export of goods to the British. At the time a considerable part of Vermont transported its surplus produce to Montreal. Suddenly this market was gone. Much of the agricultural trade with Canada remained interrupted through the War of 1812.

Natural events also contributed to the decline of Vermont and New Hampshire's farming. In the summer of 1811 a severe rain storm passed from east to west across the center of Vermont, causing widespread flooding. Bridges, barns, mills, trees, and even large boulders were swept away, and many meadows were stripped of their topsoil. In Rutland and Windsor, two of the state's most productive counties, an estimated two-thirds of all mills were washed away. An even greater blow to the area's agriculture was the "cold season" of 1816. The year is variously referred to as "the cold year," "the famine year," and "eighteen hundred and froze to death." In 1816 a severe frost came on the night of June 8, followed by a snowfall of several inches. Ice formed on ponds, the leaves froze on trees and most crops were ruined throughout both states. The cold weather did not cease in June. In one region or another the frost returned throughout the summer, and snow fell in every month that year. Although these setbacks greatly hindered the area's growth in the early part of the nineteenth century, they were less significant than deep-seated economic and social troubles. The real problem was that changes in farming had begun to make agriculture in Vermont and New Hampshire unprofitable. If a market-oriented agriculture had been viable in the area, then the difficulties experienced between the years 1808 and 1820 could have been surmounted.

At the beginning of the nineteenth century, farming in the United States underwent a major transformation, shifting from a largely self-sufficient operation to a commercial, market-oriented one. Although farmers had always grown small surpluses which were exchanged for goods in the cities, they now began to specialize in certain crops. Large amounts of a few crops were grown to be sold in ever more distant markets, made possible by improved transportation systems after the Revolutionary War. With money earned from the sale of crops and livestock, farmers began to purchase an increasing variety of manufactured goods.

The age of the self-sufficient farmer was coming to an end.

For the farmer to purchase manufactured goods, there had to be an increased availability of such goods. During the years 1815 to 1840, as America's economy began to shift from an agrarian base to an industrial one, many small factories were established in southern New England. Within a relatively short time their products were being sold to farmers in the north. The result was that the farmers needed more cash to purchase the goods they wanted.

With the passing of the age of self-sufficiency, many hillside farms of Vermont and New Hampshire no longer proved economical. They were too small for growing large surpluses, the season was too short, the land was too rocky, and most farms were too isolated for easy transportation of farm produce to distant markets. Gradually farms at higher altitudes were abandoned, and town populations shifted downward to the valleys. At the same time, more and more farmers abandoned their New England farms and moved westward.

Better land to the west was the incentive, and a great many in Vermont and New Hampshire left. Lewis Stilwell found in his study *Migration from Vermont* that by 1850 over 100,000 Vermonters had gone west, to New York, Ohio, Indiana, Michigan, Illinois, Wisconsin, and Iowa. Most who moved west continued a life of farming, but the land they now plowed was far more productive than the rocky hillsides they had left behind.

The coming of the railroads brought hope that the area's agricultural and population decline might be stemmed. In 1848 the *Farmers' Monthly Visitor* reported confidently: "The farms of central Vermont are wakening up to their true interest. The new railroad passing by them will add fifty to one hundred percent at once to the productive value of labor to all those within twenty miles of its reach." Railroads in northern New England did cut the cost of marketing in

half, but they proved to be a mixed blessing for Vermont and New Hampshire farmers. When the railroads connected southern New England with the farming regions of western New York and the Midwest, the New England market was suddenly open to a large influx of cheap agricultural products. The Vermont and New Hampshire farmers, raising grain crops on small, rocky fields, could not compete. The railroads had another unexpected result. They provided a cheaper, faster way to emigrate out of the area, and a large portion of the population did just that. By 1860 an estimated 42 percent of all Vermonters in the United States were living outside Vermont.

Many feared that the end of self-sufficient farming and the massive emigration from the area heralded the end of agriculture in the two states. Such was not the case. In the 1820s adjustments to the new realities of commercial farming had already begun. Seeking a single, viable agricultural commodity which had a chance to compete against larger farms to the west, many Vermont and New Hampshire farmers turned to sheep.

Prior to the War of 1812 many farmers in the Upper Valley and elsewhere in Vermont and New Hampshire had begun to depend on the sale of wool for their livelihood, but this first venture with

View of Randolph, Vermont, farm heavily grazed by Merino sheep, 1870s. Courtesy Special Collections, Bailey/Howe Library.

Five champion Merino rams. Etching, by Luther Allison Webster. Courtesy Vermont Historical Society.

sheep raising was short-lived. At the conclusion of the war, American markets were opened to foreign wools and woolens, with the result that many domestic woolen factories closed and the price of wool dropped considerably. Sheep raising in the two states degenerated for a period, due to overcrowding, underfeeding, and careless breeding. But this decline was brief. The introduction of improved machinery and the growth of mills in southern New England created a renewed demand for wool, and in the 1820s the area experienced a sheep-raising boom.

Raising sheep in the hill country was in many respects a natural development. Although the rugged terrain was not suitable for producing large crops, it was ideal for sheep. In the latter half of the 1830s the entire hill country of northern New England became gripped by what was termed "the sheep mania." In four years the number of sheep in Vermont increased over 50 percent, leaping from a reported 1,099,011 sheep in 1836 to 1,681,819 sheep in 1840. During the same four-year period New Hampshire experienced a similar dramatic increase in its number of sheep, jumping from approximately 465,000 to 617,390. In 1840 New Hampshire had two and one-quarter sheep for every inhabitant, while Ver-

mont counted five and three-quarters sheep for every person in that state.

According to Harold Wilson in *The Hill Country of Northern New England*, every town in Vermont — except for a few remote districts in the Green Mountains and the far northeast — had in 1840 more than a thousand sheep. Some towns had over five thousand sheep, and in the Champlain and Connecticut River Valleys a few towns contained more than ten thousand. To a lesser degree the same was true in New Hampshire. Sheep raising here was most important in the Upper Valley, where three towns — Hanover, Lebanon, and Walpole — counted over ten thousand sheep apiece. Twenty other New Hampshire towns each had over five thousand sheep.

Of the more than two million sheep in Vermont and New Hampshire in the mid-nineteenth century the great majority were Merino. Originally from Spain, where they had been bred and developed for centuries, Merino were once owned solely by the Spanish nobility. Until the early nineteenth century they were not allowed to be exported from Spain, under penalty of death. Europe's Napoleonic Wars finally undermined Spain's control over the Merino sheep when, at the beginning of the nineteenth century, France invaded Spain. In the ensuing strife, flocks were seized by both the Spanish and French governments and sold abroad.

A number of people imported from one to four Merino sheep into the United States around the beginning of the nineteenth century, but the person who contributed most to the introduction and breeding of the Spanish Merino in Vermont was William Jarvis. Serving as the American consul-general in Lisbon, Portugal, between 1802 and 1810, Jarvis arranged to buy a large number of Merinos. It is generally thought that Jarvis imported a large flock of pure-blooded Spanish Merinos, four hundred of which he took with him in 1811 to Weathersfield, Vermont.

Over the years Jarvis and many others developed the Merino strain, and in the hill country the Merino grew to be larger and hardier than its Spanish ancestor. Eventually the Vermont and New Hampshire Merino also developed a heavy yolk — a greasy secretion covering the fleece to a depth of an eighth of an inch. Some of this yolk remained after washing, and since wool was sold by weight, the demand for the heavily fleeced Merinos with their excessive secretion of yolk was very high.

The sheep boom continued into the mid-1840s, giving many the feeling that sheep would remain primary in the area's agriculture forever. In 1845, for example, the *Farmers' Monthly Visitor* prophesied, ''Careful management will always make sure the success of the fine wool growers upon the granite hills of New Hampshire.'' Ironically, just as this glowing assessment was being made, many sheep farmers were experiencing difficulties.

Between the years 1840 and 1850 the number of sheep in Vermont dropped from its high of 1,681,819 to 1,014,122. New Hampshire experienced a similar steep decline from 617,390 to 384,756. This decline continued in the following decades, and by 1870 Vermont's sheep industry had shrunk 64 percent from its zenith in 1840. During the same period the number of sheep in New Hampshire declined 59 percent.

One reason for the decline was an 1841 lowering of protective tariffs on wool. Northern New England farmers bitterly opposed the lowering, and in 1842 they did receive a temporary respite when high tariffs were reinstated. But when, in 1846, all tariffs were removed from the higher grades of wool, many farmers found themselves in permanent trouble. The price of wool plummeted, making wool production unprofitable for many. In 1848 and 1849 a widespread slaughter of sheep occurred, as farmers asked whatever price the hides and mutton would bring. The heyday of sheep raising in Vermont and New Hampshire was over.

A second factor contributing to the decline of sheep raising in the hill country was the gradual increase of wool production in the West. Until the 1840s western states produced wool primarily for home needs. With the completion of the Ohio and Pennsylvania canal systems between 1832 and 1834, the situation began to change. By the beginning of 1840, increased quantities of wool were being shipped eastward via the Erie Canal. Sheep could be raised far more cheaply in the open range areas of the West than on the rocky mountainsides in Vermont and New Hampshire. Prior to 1860, for example, the average cost per year of keeping one sheep in the East was between one and two dollars. By contrast, that cost in the Midwest and West was between twenty-five cents and one dollar.

Despite the large decline in sheep numbers, wool production in Vermont and New Hampshire remained relatively stable into the 1870s. Careful breeding had more than tripled the average weight of wool sheared per sheep, making it possible for some sheep farmers to maintain a profit even as competition from western states increased. Vermont farmers were especially successful in breeding. The Vermont Merino was, in fact, so coveted in the latter half of the nineteenth century that New York sheep were frequently shipped into Vermont and then sold as Vermont strain. Another common deception was the application of the ''Cornwall finish'' — a mixture of burnt umber, lampblack, and linseed oil. This was applied to inferior sheep, giving their fleece the color characteristic of highly bred Vermont Merino. The "finish" was virtually undetectable. The sheep were sold to unsuspecting western farmers, who only discovered they had been duped after the first rain.

For a period sheep breeding was very lucrative, providing an alternative way for many sheep farmers to stay in business. In the 1860s wool growers from all over America and from foreign countries sent to the hill country — and especially to Vermont — for Merinos as breeders. An average ram sold for eight hundred dollars, and as much as thirty-five hundred to five thousand dollars was reported for an extra-fine ram. The charge for the service of the top rams was two to three thousand dollars a season. Extra-fine ewes were sold for one to three hundred dollars.

Although breeding and increased wool production helped sustain Vermont and New Hampshire sheep farming through the turn of the century, it was a declining industry. Its final bloom came during the Civil War. When the war started, shipments of cotton from the South practically ceased, resulting in an increased demand for wool and woolen cloth. At its zenith, the price of wool during the Civil War reached one dollar per pound, and in some Vermont towns the number of sheep doubled. At the close of the war, however, cotton was again plentiful and the price of wool dropped. Large imports of wool from Australia, South America, and South Africa also began to offer extensive competition to all American wool producers.

A new factor hastened the decline in sheep raising in Vermont and New Hampshire. In the 1870s dogs began to ravage sheep flocks in large numbers. The problem became so severe that farmers substantially reduced their flocks to sizes which could be more easily guarded. Toward the end of the century, reimbursments from public funds were made to farmers whose sheep had been killed by dogs, but never in amounts large enough to fully cover the damages. Oftentimes, too, town sheep funds were insufficient when a farmer lost most of his flock.

Sheep raising continued to decline, and by 1910 only eighty-four thousand sheep remained in the entire state of Vermont. Accompanying the decline was a shift from wool bearing sheep to mutton breeds. The decline continued well into the twentieth century.

Sheep farmers discussing their rams. County fairs got their start to settle the sometimes heated disputes as to who had the best animal. Courtesy Vermont Historical Society.

The Northern Railroad

Nothing in its history transformed the Upper Valley as much as the advent of railroads. First to reach the Upper Valley was the Northern Railroad, whose tracks were opened from Concord to Lebanon on Wednesday, November 17, 1847. The following spring a railroad bridge across the Connecticut River was completed, and in June 1848 trains began making regular trips between Concord and White River Junction. A new era had come to the Upper Valley.

Talk of trains to the region had started at a very early date. In November 1827 a letter published in the *New Hampshire Statesman & Concord Register* first suggested that a railroad be constructed from Concord to the confluence of the White and Connecticut Rivers. The suggestion must have seemed fanciful to many at the time. The first steam locomotive in America did not run until two years later, on August 8, 1829, in eastern Pennsylvania, and then only briefly. It was found to be too heavy for the rigid track. By 1832 there were only thirty-two miles of track in the entire United States.

Talk of a railroad to the Upper Valley continued, and within fifteen years the suggestion made in 1827 no longer seemed improbable. By 1840 railroad mileage in the United States had increased to 2,818 miles. Two years later

the Concord Railroad passed northward through the Merrimack valley as far as Concord. An extension of this line to the Upper Valley was a distinct possibility, and if politics had not suddenly intruded, a railroad might have reached the area before 1847.

Fearful that both the Concord and the Nashua and Lowell Railroads might control all trade to the north country, New Hampshire politicians passed a law in 1842 that railroad construction could proceed only after a landowner was paid whatever he demanded for land over which tracks were to pass. Railroad construction in New Hamsphire temporarily ceased. Opposition to this law surfaced immediately in the Upper Valley and other parts of the state. In Lebanon a special convention of the "friends of internal improvements in New Hampshire" was held in 1843. The purpose of the gathering was to generate popular enthusiasm for a railroad connecting the existing lines at Concord with proposed Vermont lines that would converge at White River Junction. The principal organizer of this convention was Charles Haddock, a professor of political economy at Dartmouth College. Addressing those present, Haddock asserted that "the most urgent, immediate want of New Hampshire, is — PUBLIC ROADS for Travel and Transportation. . . ." These roads were "to connect the State with those parts of the adjacent States with which we have most intercourse, so that our commerce and communication with those States may be MOST CONVENIENT and LUCRATIVE to us."

Moved by public pressure, the New Hampshire legislature revoked the law of 1842, and in 1844 it granted the railroads the right to take land for right of way by virtue of eminent domain. That same year the Northern Railroad was granted a charter, empowering its incorporators to "construct and keep in use a Rail-Road . . . running by such route as shall be deemed best to accomodate the public" from Concord to the west bank of the Connecticut River in Lebanon.

Surveys for the railroad began late in 1842 and were completed in 1844. Beginning in Concord, the route accepted was to pass through nine towns, finally ending in Lebanon, a distance of seventy

miles. Aware of the commercial benefits of a railroad, the towns along the line welcomed its construction — except the Enfield Shakers. The proposed route of the Northern Railroad was supposed to pass on the south side of Mascoma Lake and run through the Shaker village. The Shakers opposed this route and donated land on the north side of Mascoma Lake, where the railroad was built.

Construction of the Northern Railroad was relatively rapid. Built largely by laborers who had left Ireland during the potato famines of the 1840s, the line reached from Concord to Franklin by December 28, 1846. In July 1847 the tracks were completed to Andover, and then to Grafton in early September. Two months later the rails reached Lebanon. The *Granite State Whig* noted that on November 17 over twelve hundred stockholders and invited guests traveled with the Northern Railroad to Lebanon, "where appropriate ceremonies of the occasion took place."

The "appropriate ceremonies" included lengthy speeches by Daniel Webster, former Governor Charles Paine of Vermont and Mayor Josiah Phillips Quincy of Boston. Charles T. Russell of Boston also spoke, stating: "We have threaded our quiet way over and through the hills, from the valley of the Merrimac itself. . . . We have carved a passage through the rock, leveled the hills and filled the valleys. We have moved . . . more than 3,354,000 cubic yards of earth. . . . We have moved more than 87,000 yards of solid rock, and have constructed 64,854 perches of bridge and culvert masonry. We have spanned the Connecticut, and opened the modern steam highway from New Hampshire's Western to her central river. In this we have expended about $2,000,000."

Trains on the Northern Railroad left Concord at 10:30 A.M. and 3:00 P.M.; from West Lebanon the trains left at 7:05 A.M. and 12:55 P.M. A ticket from Lebanon to Concord cost $1.75, and from Lebanon to Boston the price was $3.25. Traveling at an average speed of twenty-three miles per hour, the full day stage trip from Leb-

Promotional piece for the Northern Railroad, 1845. Courtesy Baker Library.

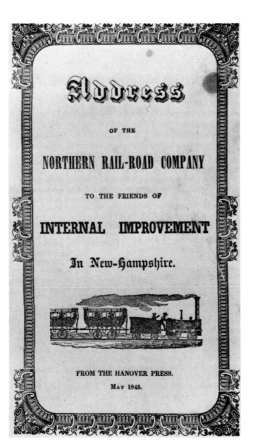

Address

OF THE

NORTHERN RAIL-ROAD COMPANY

TO THE FRIENDS OF

INTERNAL IMPROVEMENT

In New-Hampshire.

FROM THE HANOVER PRESS.
MAY 1845.

110

Woodstock Railroad founded in 1875

0 10 20 30 40
miles

LONG DISTANCE

RAILROAD NETWORK OF

NORTHERN NEW ENGLAND

1847-1852

anon to Concord was reduced to a matter of hours. The trip from Lebanon to Boston, which took six days at the time of the Revolutionary War, could now be completed in less than one day.

A substantially reduced traveling time was not the only difference the Northern Railroad made. Unlike the rivers and roads, which were often im-passable during periods of cold or bad weather, the trains ran daily with little disruption between the various towns. The semi-isolation of the Upper Valley was coming to an end.

The area's isolation disappeared completely as other lines reached into the Upper Valley. In 1849 the Cheshire Railroad extended through Keene and up

111

to Bellows Falls, Vermont. The same year tracks were laid from Bellows Falls up the Connecticut River on the New Hampshire side. The line passed through Charlestown and Claremont and over to Windsor, which was already connected with White River Junction. By 1850 tracks ran the entire length of the Connecticut River from the southern border of Vermont to St. Johnsbury.

The Northern Railroad and other railroads immediately replaced all other modes of transportation to the Upper Valley. River traffic on the Connecticut ceased completely, and the Concord coaches which had carried passengers over the turnpikes were now used to transport passengers and baggage from train stations to hotels. Other changes were introduced as well. Earlier, the primary concern had been to establish an improved transportation route from Boston or Hartford to the Upper Valley. This was achieved with the railroads, but at the same time people now wished to connect the Upper Valley with different commercial centers, such as Ogdensburg, New York and Montreal. Trade routes had ceased to be defined in terms of the Connecticut River or any other geographical factor.

The desire to join the Upper Valley with Montreal was particularly strong, and even before the Northern Railroad was complete to Lebanon, plans were being made to go on to Montreal. Reasons for the interest in Montreal were multiple, but essentially they centered on the question of how raw materials from Canada could best be transported to Europe and how finished goods from Europe could be returned to Canada. In the 1840s these goods were shipped largely through the St. Lawrence waterway which, like the rivers and canals of northern New England, was frozen in the winter.

Added stimulus for building a railroad to Montreal came in 1846, when the British Parliament repealed its Corn Laws, which had restricted the imports of wheat, grain, and other foodstuffs into England. That same year the American Congress passed an act allowing Canadian imports and exports to pass through the United States without duties. Sensing commercial possibilities, the directors of the Northern Railroad began to encourage the completion of Canadian

The Northern Railroad Engine No. 8, the Grafton, about 1872. The station is believed to be Newbury, New Hampshire, on the Northern-controlled Concord and Claremont Railroad line. Courtesy NEW ENGLAND RAIL SERVICE.

112

railroads from Montreal to the United States.

In 1851, barely three years after the opening of the Northern Railroad to Lebanon, a line was opened to Montreal. In traveling the route, trains passed over the rails of seven different railroad companies, including four between Boston and the Connecticut River. Nevertheless, Boston was now connected with Montreal via the Upper Valley. Opening of the railroad to Montreal contributed greatly to the Upper Valley. For many years the Northern Railroad played a part in the transportation of Canadian wheat south to Boston, where it was then loaded on steamships and sent to Europe. The same railroad route was also used by the British government to convey official Canadian mail.

Apart from the immediate commercial advantages, the Northern Railroad and other lines created a basis for future changes in the Upper Valley. Towns like Lebanon and White River Junction, situated on a major transportation route between Montreal and Boston, suddenly had access to world markets. Goods carried to Boston by rail could then be shipped by steamship to England, reaching their final destination in under three weeks.

This ready access to world markets transformed Upper Valley towns like Lebanon and Claremont from agricultural communities to industrial ones. The arrival of the Northern Railroad encouraged the construction of mills and factories along the Mascoma River in the center of Lebanon. After the Civil War, when railroads were improved by the introduction of steel rails and better trains, industrial development rapidly expanded along the Mascoma River in Lebanon and the Sugar River in Claremont.

Until well after World War II, the Northern Railroad continued to serve the Upper Valley as a primary transportation route to Boston. By then it was no longer known to most people as the Northern Railroad, but rather as the Boston & Maine. In 1890, the Northern Railroad was consolidated through a ninety-nine-year leasing agreement with the Boston & Maine — a system which by then covered most of New Hampshire. Its name is rarely heard today, but the Northern Railroad still continues as an independent company by virtue of its leasing agreements. And although they are no longer used, the rails of this first railroad to the Upper Valley are still in place.

WRECK OF THE CENTRAL VERMONT

SATURDAY, February 5, 1887. The Central Vermont Railroad Night Express left the White River Junction depot at 2:10 A.M. and headed north. Pulling a baggage car, a combined mail and smoker car, two passenger cars, and two sleepers was the forty-five ton locomotive E.H. Baker. Aboard were eighty-eight passengers, including a crew of eleven. Outside the temperature had dropped to eighteen degrees below zero. To ward off the cold, the coal stoves in the passenger

cars had been freshly stoked at White River Junction.

Eight minutes after departure from the White River Junction depot, the train began to slow as it approached the curve into the White River Bridge — then called the Woodstock Bridge. The train started over the bridge. "Suddenly," a passenger named Tewksbury later recalled, "we felt a swaying of the car back and forth, and a jolting, and I knew the wheels were running along the sleepers [ties]." Both

THE BRIDGE AND CARS IN FLAMES.

Scene of the 1887 wreck of the Central Vermont's Night Express. HARPER'S WEEKLY, *February 1887.*

Tewksbury and a conductor grabbed the bell cord, and the engineer, hearing the alarm, immediately applied the airbrakes. It did not help. The rear end of the last sleeper car was already swinging off the bridge. When it fell from the bridge, it pulled the other sleeper and the two passenger cars with it. The coupling broke between the mail car and the first passenger car, allowing the front part of the train to escape the ensuing disaster.

The four wooden train cars fell forty-three feet, smashing onto thick ice. All four cars collapsed on impact, trapping most of the passengers inside. Within minutes, the four cars burst into flames, set afire by the coal stoves and the sperm oil lamps. The train crew grabbed all available tools and hurried down to help. They scarcely knew where to start. Agonizing screams came from everywhere. One woman recalled: "From the cars I could hear the most terrible cries, piercing the very soul. One voice still rings in my ears. It was that of another woman, who kept crying, "Won't someone let me out?""

Several were saved, but within minutes the cars were a sheet of flames. Others who might have been saved died in the blaze, their bodies so badly burned that an exact death toll was never established. Officials guessed that thirty died in the accident; thirty-seven others were injured, out of a passenger list of eighty-eight.

An official investigation concluded that the accident occurred when a rail broke under the weight of the train in the extreme cold. The broken rail then threw the passenger cars off the tracks before they reached the bridge. Investigators also determined that "the defect in the rail could not have been discovered before it broke." But even though the accident probably could not have been prevented, safety measures could have been taken. "There is no doubt, however," the investigating commission added, "that many who lost their lives in the accident would have been saved if it had not been for the stoves and lights in the wrecked cars."

The absence of safety measures on the Night Express was common. During this period numerous train accidents occurred, and often the major ones were directly or indirectly the result of a cost-saving measure at the expense of safety. By 1887, for example, several railroads used electric lighting in place of kerosene or oil lamps. Many railroads also used steam from the engines to heat the cars. The means for preventing conflagrations after train wrecks were available.

The bridge disaster at the White River — at the time the third largest train wreck in the United States — created a national uproar. A call for improved safety followed, and finally in 1893 the Railway Appliance Act was passed by Congress, establishing for the first time national safety requirements for all railroad equipment. The law eliminated many of the unnecessarily dangerous aspects of railroad travel.

THE WOOSTOCK RAILROAD

WHEN THEY first arrived in the Upper Valley, railroads seemed to offer unlimited possibilities. One grandiose reaction was the 1847 projection of a transcontinental railroad, the Atlantic & Pacific Railway, to run from Portland, Maine, through Vermont, and from there to "all the West." A survey map of the proposed route showed the line running through Woodstock, Vermont.

When the survey map appeared, Woodstock's three thousand residents were greatly excited. Edgar Mead, in his book *Over the Hills to Woodstock*, nar-

The 1875 test run of the Winooski over the bridge spanning Quechee Gorge. Courtesy Woodstock Historical Society.

rates the events that followed. A group was quickly organized to plan the segment of the transcontinental railroad through Woodstock, Bridgewater, and on to Rutland. A charter was granted by the Vermont legislature, but nothing happened. Funds could not be raised and the charter expired.

Despite the initial setback, the magnificient idea of a transcontinental railroad through Vermont remained alive. In October 1863 a new charter was granted, incorporating the Woodstock Railroad Company. Again, nothing happened. In 1867 talk of "on to the West" resurfaced, and Woodstock once more actively prepared to build. This time enough money was collected to begin construction in April 1868.

Work on the Woodstock Railroad was rapid. Twenty-one crews with 350 men were employed, and by January 1869 eight miles of the fourteen-mile line had been graded. By September grading was nearly complete, but then the bottom fell out. Beset by financial difficulties, the Woodstock Railroad halted construction in March 1870, unable to begin again for over four years.

In the summer of 1874 work on the Woodstock Railroad recommenced, and this time construction continued until the following summer, when the line was finished. A wooden lattice bridge was built over the Quechee Gorge, and on September 29, 1875, the first train from White River Junction arrived in Woodstock. At long last the Woodstock Railroad was completed. There remained only the extension to "all the West," but that dream never became reality. Talk of an Atlantic & Pacific Railway from Portland, Maine, vanished, and the fourteen miles of the Woodstock Railroad led no farther. The line was not even extended the few miles westward to Bridgewater, although that town had contributed forty thousand dollars to the building of the railroad.

Because the line led nowhere, the Woodstock Railroad remained financially shaky for several years. Only when Woodstock became a fashionable resort at the end of the nineteenth century, did the railroad enjoy its first success. Reorganized in 1890 as the Woodstock Railway, the line carried Pullman and parlor cars from Boston and New York, tranporting the wealthy to Woodstock, with its recently invented Sanatoga Springs and its newly constructed Woodstock Inn. But the period of elegance was short-lived. By 1916 service was so reduced that one crew could handle all trains. The decline continued through the 1920s, and by 1931 the railroad's finances were so reduced that maintenance of the trains and track beds was practically eliminated. Permission to abandon the line was obtained, and on April 15, 1933, the Woodstock Railway made its final run. Today the asphalt surface of Route 4 passes over much of the railroad's former route.

Early Mills of Lebanon

THE DECLINE of self-sufficient farming in the Upper Valley, accompanied by a simultaneous rise of industry, resulted in major shifts in town populations. The once rather even population distribution throughout the landscape was altered, as farms grew larger to accomodate sheep or were simply abandoned as unprofitable. Populations began to concentrate in communities on or near major waterfalls, where by the mid-nineteenth century a variety of mills began to flourish.

These shifts not only meant that many towns lost in population while others increased; major changes within townships themselves also occurred. Sections originally settled in a town, or areas fairly densely populated often declined or were completely abandoned, as populations shifted toward newly developed waterways. The railroads often contributed to these shifts.

Lebanon is a perfect example of a town in the Upper Valley where development and growth were strongly influenced by both the presence of rapids and the advent of railroads. Located directly on the Connecticut River, the town was originally settled in the east and west parts of the township. There, in what became known as West Lebanon and East Lebanon (where the Mascoma River flows out of Mascoma Lake), the first saw and grist mills were built. Lebanon's first industry also developed there, and through the 1820s and 1830s the major part of the town's population was in West and East Lebanon.

In the 1840s industry and population in both West and East Lebanon began to decline, as the focus of the town shifted to its center. The shift occurred because of the Mascoma River and the Northern Railroad. In the center of Lebanon the Mascoma River begins a rapid drop of

seventy feet, providing a tremendous amount of waterpower. The railroad had to come, however, before this waterpower could be utilized fully. As long as transportation by water remained primary, West Lebanon, located on the Connecticut River, and East Lebanon, located at Mascoma Lake, were more suitable for settlement. At both places dams were built, which provided sufficient power for the first mills.

With railroads it was no longer important that an industry be located directly on a large navigable river, such as the Connecticut. Large quantities of products could easily be transported into and out of the center of Lebanon. Full advantage of the tremendous waterpower on the Mascoma River could be taken, and larger mills could be built. Eventually a series of five dams were built on the Mascoma, and mills and shops were built on both sides of the river.

One of the first persons to establish an industry on this center site was a man by the name of Mahan, who around 1830 built a small shop in which he made agricultural tools. Eventually Mahan's business outgrew this shop, and he sold it sometime in the 1840s to Martin Buck. In 1847 the Northern Railroad arrived, and Buck's shop began to expand. In 1848 Buck began to advertise in the *Granite State Whig* that he had purchased the right to make and sell ''Platt's Patent Grist Mill.'' The advertised advantages of this grist mill lay in the fact that its stone was lighter than others and could therefore be turned faster and easier. How long Buck continued to sell grist mills is uncertain.

Buck's shop manufactured more than grist mills. It was an iron foundry — later an iron and brass foundry — making machinery to be used in making other

machinery. The Buck Foundry sold its products to other parts of the world, and it is believed that it made some of the machinery used in England to manufacture the Enfield rifle in the 1850s.

By 1860 the Buck Foundry was the largest industry in Lebanon, employing 100 to 150 people. Just why the Buck Foundry ceased operations is unclear, but in the latter part of the 1860s the upper shops were sold to Sturtevant Manufacturing. Under Sturtevant, the foundry disappeared, and in its place developed an extensive and renowned woodworking business. Sturtevant manufactured house finish and furniture for the Victorian period. It made, among other things, elaborate mouldings for exteriors, door entrances, window sashes, and ornate wooden mantels for fireplaces. It also produced many pieces of heavy Victorian furniture with elaborately carved designs.

For unknown reasons Sturtevant failed financially in 1876, and was subsequently taken over by two men named Mead and Mason. Mead, Mason, & Co. continued the woodworking business and expanded it. The company moved into the lower shops as well, where it had paint shops for the furniture it manufactured. On the opposite side of the Mascoma River was a warehouse for the storage of completed furniture and house finish. Robert Leavitt, Lebanon's current town historian, believes that in the 1880s Mead, Mason, & Co. employed as many as three hundred workers. If true, the company employed close to one-half of Lebanon's industrial workers.

In the 1870s, along with the woodworking industry, a great many other mills and shops came to be located in the center area of Lebanon. There was the shop of Webb and Sawyer, which manufactured wooden lamps, sleds, and wheelbarrows. It opened in 1878 and at the time employed ten people. Around the same time H.P. Goodrich had a small shop as a stair and rail builder. Another industry existing for many years in Leb-

The Sturtevant Manufacturing Company's lower shops on the Mascoma River, 1873. Note two of the five falls to the left upriver, as well as the bridges. Courtesy Lebanon Historical Society.

119

anon was the manufacture of agricultural equipment. In East Lebanon there was the Emerson Scythe Factory, which later moved to the center part of Lebanon and located near another scythe factory begun by Stephan D. Slayton in 1845. N.B. Marston was another manufacturer of agricultural equipment. He and his sons produced an adjustable drag rake and also made snow shovels. In addition there was the Granite Agricultural Works, which came to Lebanon in 1872. Thirty people were employed here in making plows and mowing machines. This company, plagued by fires, burned in 1873 and 1875.

The manufacture of agricultural equipment was a part of a prominent and diverse industry in Lebanon — metalwork. In addition to Buck's foundry, there were several other foundries, including the Purmort Foundry and the foundry of Cole, Bugbee & Leavitt, later S. Cole & Son, which made castings and did a large amount of mill work. And there was the shop of C.M. Baxter, which manufactured band saws and woodworking machines.

To this industry of metalwork belonged also Kendrick, Davis & Co. — the one company begun in Lebanon in the nineteenth century which still continues to operate, today as K&D. Originally located in the center of town, it was called the ''keyshop'' because it first manufactured keys used to wind up watches. It was a thriving business, producing what was called the ''Dust Proof Watch Key.'' This was a key constructed with an open part to allow dust or pocket lint to pass through. Later Kendrick, Davis & Co. made watchmakers' and jewelers' tools, becoming internationally known for their work.

Although woodworking and metalwork were the two most prominent industries in Lebanon through the 1870s and into the 1880s, there were many other shops as well. There was, for example, the Shepard Organ Co., which in 1873 employed twenty-two people. Carriages were also made in Lebanon, as were mops. In the early days of West Lebanon there was a brick works, and in the lat-

ter part of the nineteenth century a boot and shoe company existed for a short time in the center of town.

One of the most unusual factories in Lebanon was the Sponge Factory, which came there shortly after the Civil War and initially employed thirty to forty workers. The Sponge Factory did not make sponges. Ocean sponge was shipped by rail to Lebanon, and in the Sponge Factory it was shredded and processed to produce elastic sponge. This was then used in upholstery, mattresses, cushions, and in anything else for which horsehair was used. It was the precursor of foam rubber, and for several years the Sponge Factory was a large operation. Housed in a building five stories high, the factory was capable of manufacturing two tons of sponge per day. Eventually the Sponge Factory failed, because sponge proved to be a poor substitute for horsehair since it absorbed water and lost its elasticity over time.

By 1887 most of Lebanon's industry was concentrated in the center of the town. Six hundred workers were employed in the various mills and shops. Then in one night the entire mill area burned to the ground. It was shortly after midnight on Tuesday, May 10, 1887, when a fire broke out in Mead, Mason & Co.'s lower shop. Within a short time the fire spread across the road through a connecting covered overhead bridge and began to burn the Mead, Mason & Co. warehouse. Fanned by winds, the fire moved up to the upper shops and rapidly spread to other mills. Before the fire was brought under control, eighty buildings were burned to the ground.

Reconstruction of the mill area in the center of Lebanon began shortly after the fire, but there was never again the same concentration and variety of industry. Woodworking rapidly diminished in importance as the Victorian period began to wane. Demand for the house finish and furniture manufactured by Mead, Mason & Co. declined, and in 1890 Mead and Mason sold their buildings to the Everitt Knitting Works. Lebanon's center now began to depend on the woolen industry — the industry which was going to dominate Lebanon and the Upper Valley through the first half of the twentieth century.

The woolen industry first came to Lebanon before the fire, when in 1882 woolen mills were established on Mechanic Street. Called the Mascoma Mills, they originally manufactured flannel. In 1888, the year after the great fire, a second woolen mill opened in Lebanon. This was the Lebanon Woolen Mill, started by Carter and Rogers and built on the site where the Sponge Factory had once stood. The Lebanon Woolen Mill initially manufactured shoddy — a cheap reprocessed woolen cloth. A third mill, the Riverside Woolen Co., opened in 1893.

By the close of the nineteenth century Lebanon's major industries were wool and clothing, which continued to expand until by the1920s there were one thousand workers employed at the three woolen mills and the Everett Knitting Works. Lebanon's woolen mills generally manufactured material for men's suits and overcoats, while the Everett Knitting Works primarily made clothing of jersey and orlon. The dominance achieved by these industries in Lebanon by the end of the nineteenth century was seen in towns throughout the Upper Valley, and in other parts of northern New England as well. The shift from the woodworking and metal industries to wool brought considerable changes. Larger companies devoted only to the production of woolen goods replaced the many small and diverse mills and shops of the nineteenth century. Skilled handwork, necessary in the metal and woodworking industries, was also generally eliminated. The age of routine labor had arrived.

After the 1887 fire, Lebanon. The walls and chimney of the one building still standing are the remains of the S. Cole & Son foundry. Courtesy Lebanon Historical Society.

EAST AND WEST LEBANON

WHAT CAN BE called Lebanon's first industrial community developed shortly after the end of the Revolutionary War in East Lebanon. Here, at the foot of Mascoma Lake, Elisha Payne built a large saw and wood-finishing mill, which in all likelihood cut the lumber for the first Dartmouth College buildings. Started in 1780, almost nothing is known of Payne's mill. In 1840 the mill burned, and in its place was built the Haskell Furniture Shops. There is no record of Haskell's beginning, but it is known to have existed into the 1870s. The Haskell Furniture Shops initially produced what were called Windsor benches. These were natural wood benches used in almost every church and town hall in the area. Later Haskell manufactured mainly school furniture.

Lumber and furniture remained principal industries throughout most of East Lebanon's limited history. Wool was also important. One of the first carding and cloth works in northern New England was located here in the mid-nineteenth century. Later there was a bobbin mill as well, which produced bobbins for the nearby woolen mills. In the latter part of the nineteenth century, a small metal industry began in East Lebanon when one of Lebanon's scythe factories was built there. East Lebanon also had two hotels and enough three story rooming houses to board the two, possibly three hundred workers employed nearby.

Today barely a trace testifies that East Lebanon ever existed. In the 1840s the settlement began to decline, and by the turn of the century it was gone.

Buildings and documents have disappeared. All that remains are a few vague recollections.

The early industrial history of West Lebanon is equally unclear. Sometime in the 1830s or 1840s what was called the Cambridge Mill manufactured chintz — a cotton cloth printed in various colors and usually glazed. It was a popular choice for ladies' dresses as well as for the backs of furniture. Around the same time, a fulling mill operated in West Lebanon. There, through a process of moisture, heat, and pressure, cotton cloth was sized and stiffened.

Other mills were located in West Lebanon, but little is known about them. Industry in West Lebanon was apparently never as extensive as that of East Lebanon, and it was an inn-and-tavern trade which became the major source for West Lebanon employment. The community's location at the junction of the Connecticut and White Rivers made it early an ideal layover place. A stone wharf was built at West Lebanon, and boats and river barges stopped there to unload goods, which were subsequently transported up the White River and Connecticut River.

When the railroad came to Lebanon in 1847, West Lebanon was again a crossroad. The inn trade began to diminish, however, as more goods than people passed through West Lebanon. At this time, too, West Lebanon's mills began to decline, and in the second half of the 1800s the railroad became the town's chief employer.

The Dewey Woolen Mills

AT THE TURN of the century woolen mills had been erected in numerous small towns in the Upper Valley, and wool was the dominant valley industry. Unlike dairy farming, which also became important at that time, the woolen industry has largely vanished from the Upper Valley. An empty woolen mills is a familiar sight, and in Lebanon, Enfield, Claremont, and elsewhere, the unused or converted mills are constant reminders that the woolen industry belongs to the area's past.

How extensive the woolen industry was cannot be measured by the empty buildings still standing. In addition to those remaining, many others have long since been torn down. Some of the razed mills were quite large. The Dewey Mills in Quechee, Vermont, is one example of a large and active mill which has completely disappeared. In operation for over one hundred years, it was at its height a small village of sixty-three buildings, including housing for its workers. Today virtually nothing remains of these many buildings once situated at the head of the Quechee Gorge.

The Dewey Mills was founded in July 1836 by Albert Galatin Dewey, who was born in 1805 in Hartford, Vermont. Little is known about Dewey's childhood, but when he was eighteen years old his father died, and the responsibility of providing for his family fell to him. Woodworking was at the time a widespread occupation in the area, and like many other young men he entered into an apprenticeship with a carpenter. He subsequently worked as a carpenter until 1831, when he changed jobs and became a machinist in the shop of Daniels & Co. in Woodstock. Mastering the trade of millwright within a few months, Dewey was sent out to install machinery for his new employer. He worked in this capacity for five years, gaining a comprehensive knowledge of textile machinery, which he put to personal use when, in the summer of 1836, he opened his own mill at the head of Quechee Gorge.

The site was an ideal location for a mill. A natural falls was easily dammed, and wool from the more than thirteen thousand sheep in Hartford was readily available. Despite the seemingly favorable conditions, Dewey was almost hope-

Albert Galatin Dewey.
Courtesy Baker Library.

lessly in debt after three years operation. Using only new wool from farmers within a thirty-mile radius, his production capacity was 450 yards daily. This was insufficient to meet his expenditures, and by 1839 his debt approached fifteen thousand dollars.

Dewey's main problem was transportation. In a sense he was trying to establish the woolen industry in the Upper Valley in a period when it was still unprofitable to do so. His only access to the urban markets around Boston was by wagon, and such long trips could not be made daily. A team left the mill every week with finished goods and traveled to Boston. The following week the same team returned with raw materials. This limited means of transportation to primary markets restricted output, and Dewey's costs continued to exceed what he could sell.

Because of these difficulties, the Dewey Mills would have collapsed in the first years of operation if creditors had not firmly believed in the company's potential. Further credit was extended to Dewey, and continued to be extended to him, through 1850. Dewey also adjusted to his continuous financial problems, and in 1841 he started using what was then called "rag wool" — now termed "shoddy." This was wool processed from old rags, rather than new or "virgin wool." Shoddy was cheaper than wool, and Dewey was able to reduce costs.

Special machinery was needed to tear the rags and to resolve them once again into wool. Such machinery was unavailable to Dewey in Quechee, so he commissioned Daniels & Co. to build a "shoddy picker" under his direction. When this shoddy picker was introduced in the Dewey Mills in 1841, it was the first of its kind in the United States. Throughout its history, the Dewey Mills continued to manufacture cloth from shoddy, making it the oldest mill in the country to use reworked wool.

The manufacture of rag wool helped reduce the mill's debts, but it did not solve the problems of limited transportation. Only when railroads arrived in the Upper Valley did the Dewey Mills at last develop full potential. When the first train arrived in White River Junction in 1848, success was finally assured. The weekly wagon journey to Boston was replaced by a daily trip to White River Junction, where finished goods were loaded onto trains. Production was increased accordingly, to match the capacity possible with daily shipments.

The railroad connection at White River Junction was good, but Dewey realized that more immediate access to railways would be even better. To facilitate improved connections, he became one of the major promoters of the Woodstock Railroad. When this railroad opened in September, 1875, the Dewey Mills was its principal customer. Over the years the mills remained such an important customer, that its later shift to trucking for transportation was a significant factor leading to the closing of the Woodstock Railroad in 1933.

With the advent of railroads, the Dewey Mills began to prosper for the first time. By 1856 all debts had been paid, and the company began gradually to expand. By 1870 it was producing thirteen hundred yards of material daily. Fifteen years later, in 1885, daily production had increased to two thousand yards, and the company employed about eighty workers. Throughout its history, the Dewey Mills specialized in lower-priced fabrics. Chief among these fabrics was "satinet" — a cloth of wool and cotton made to resemble satin. The Dewey Mills made the first satinet in the United States in 1839, and over the years it was well known for this specialty. By 1900 annual production had reached five hundred thousand yards of material.

A. G. Dewey actively ran the operations until his death at age eighty-one in 1886. Control of the company subsequently passed to his two sons, John and William, and in later years family ownership continued, when third and fourth generation members assumed control. In the nineteenth and early twentieth centuries, family ownership and operation was common in smaller mills and factories, which frequently were organized in a paternalistic fashion. It was not just a job offered to the workers at the mills, but an entire life structured and limited by the mill's daily operations. The Dewey Mills was no exception.

Housing, for example, was offered to workers at the Dewey Mills at very low rents. By the twentieth century there were eighteen single-, two-, three-, and four-family houses within a close radius of the mills. There was also a boarding house, with capacity to house and feed sixty workers. When the mills were not operating, no rent was charged to the workers. Garden plots were made available to the workers; in spring the company plowed the plots and in autumn picked them up. In off hours many employees worked in their gardens.

A store was operated for the workers, and flour, sugar, molasses, and other necessities were bought in large quantities to reduce costs. At one time coal was purchased by the carload and sold to the employees at wholesale. Before refrigera-

tion the company cut ice for the village houses. Until 1902 there was a school in the workers' village. The company also helped organize much of its workers' leisure time. A large wagon, able to carry twenty-six people, was built to carry Catholic employees to the church in White River Junction. There was also a company band, which traveled around to local fairs. And there was a Dewey Mills baseball team and a company gun club.

Workers employed at the Dewey Mills entered a company village, which provided for them in a broad, yet limited way. The care was extended only as long as a worker remained a part of the com-

Courtyard of the A. G. Dewey Company, 1880. A. G. Dewey is standing on the office steps, right foreground. From A. G. DEWEY COMPANY, 1836-1936. Courtesy Baker Library.

*Riding the Gertie Buck, the Woodstock Railroad inspection car,
used by the Dewey family for trips to White River Junction
and Woodstock. Courtesy Woodstock Historical Society.*

pany "family." Benefits such as pension plan were not provided, and middle-aged workers often worried about the day when they would be too old to work.

The Dewey Mills continued in operation for well over one hundred years, manufacturing a variety of materials. Like most other woolen mills in the Upper Valley, it continued production through World War II and into the 1950s, when the woolen industry of New England began a steep decline because of competition from world markets and the development of synthetic materials. In the early 1950s the Dewey Mills at the head of the Quechee Gorge closed, although for a time the company's operations continued in Enfield. For several years the mills in Quechee stood empty, as so many others do today. Construction of a flood control dam at North Hartland on the Ottauquechee River finally forced an abandonment of the site. In 1962 the mill and the many houses around it were torn down, leaving little trace of the village life that thrived there for so long.

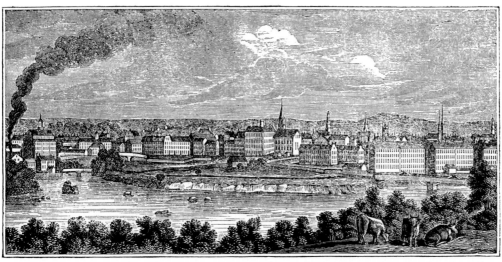

East view of Lowell, Massachusetts, 1838. Drawn by J. W. Barber, engraved by E. L. Barber.

FROM THE FARM TO THE FACTORY

MANY OF the workers in the Upper Valley woolen mills were women. In fact, in the mid-nineteenth century many women in northern New England began to leave the farms and to seek employment in newly opened textile mills just to the south. Usually a woman's motivation for leaving a rural life was the wages she could earn. Paid almost nothing for her work on the farm, a mill job gave her money to save for the future, to buy clothes she wanted, or to obtain a better education. Rarely were a woman's wages sent back home. The money a woman earned was used for herself, spent and saved as she alone saw fit.

Lowell, Massachusetts, was the first factory town to attract young women in large numbers, and, according to Thomas Dublin in *Farm to Factory*, the textile mill there employing the most women — a total of 199 — had 71 from New Hampshire, 38 from Vermont, and 39 from Maine. In another mill, where 183 women were employed, 55 were from New Hampshire, 52 from Vermont, and

45 from Maine. In every mill in Lowell the majority of women employed were from northern New England, and in many cases the proportion was as high as 75 percent. Dublin estimates that by 1845, 1200 women from Vermont alone were working in Lowell.

Through the rest of the century, women continued to leave the farm for the factory. Most frequently they were from the middle ranks of rural families, neither rich nor impoverished. Many came from large families, indicating that their departure was perhaps stimulated by a family's desire to have one less mouth to feed. The move to the mills did not sever family ties, however. In many cases relatives or close family members worked in the same mills or lived in the same town. Such kinships were steadily maintained, providing significant roles in the lives of young factory women.

At times considerable and loud opposition was expressed in northern New England about the large numbers of women entering the mills. In 1857 the

Reverend McKeen thundered at a Vermont church convention: "All great cities are cursed with immense ignorance and error, vice and crime and misery . . . far better is it for our youth to breath the pure air and enjoy the salutary moral influence of their native State, than to be brought into contact with such masses of putrefaction."

In the same year "A Farmer's Daughter" wrote a letter to the *New England Farmer*, saying she was a member of a large family and that "the respected head of our family has so many calls for his surplus funds that there is next to nothing left for the girls." In the following issue the *New England Farmer* editorialized,

unhelpfully, that the "Farmer's Daughter" should remain at home and attempt to find employment sewing or teaching in order to supplement the family's scanty resources.

The advice for women to shun the cities and factories had no effect. The United States had begun an irreversible transformation from an agricultural economy to an industrial one. Accompanying this transformation was an equally dramatic shift in the lives of women. By 1900 women composed a substantial part of the woolen mills work force in the Upper Valley and elsewhere in New England.

Women workers in one of Lebanon's woolen mills, about 1900.
Courtesy Lebanon Historical Society.

Windsor and the Machine Tool Industry

OTHER significant industries existed in the region besides wool and cloth. Most important among these was the manufacture of machine tools in Windsor and Springfield, Vermont. A major contribution was made to the development of our present-day manufacturing system based on the interchangeability of parts, when in the 1840s the small company of Robbins & Lawrence in Windsor manufactured ten thousand rifles within eighteen months.

Modern industry is unimaginable without precision machines and interchangeable parts. Yet, neither was possible without the development of modern machine tools. The importance of machine tools was realized, in a sense, at a particular historical moment in 1765, when James Watt in England resolved, in theory, the problems involved in building the first steam engine. Although he knew how to build a steam engine, he could not find the tools or workmen capable of manufacturing such a complex machine with sufficient precision. Ten years passed before a boring machine capable of producing an accurate cylinder was developed.

That inability to produce a fairly precise metal cylinder near the end of the eighteenth century is not surprising. In 1775 the tools used for cutting metal resembled those used in the Middle Ages. The principal parts in all machinery were made of wood, and only the fastenings and smaller parts were of metal. These were cast, or forged and fitted by hand. After 1775 machine tools changed rapidly.

Most modern machine tools were developed in England and the United States between 1800 and 1850. General machine tools — including the boring machine, planer, and steam hammer — were essentially developed in England, whereas the special machine tools — including milling machines and automatic lathes — were developed in America. In the United States the development of an interchangeable system of manufacturing introduced such important innovations that it constituted a second phase of the Industrial Revolution.

The idea of interchangeability first originated in Europe, where for years various countries had hoped to develop a rifle with interchangeable parts. Such a weapon would provide a distinct advantage to the army which possessed it. Earlier in the century attempts to do this had been made, and in the United States a high degree of success had been achieved. Simeon North, for example, contracted with the United States government in 1813 to manufacture pistols with component parts "to correspond so exactly that any limb or part of one pistol may be fitted to any other pistol of the Twenty Thousand." North's factory in Middletown, Connecticut, was successful in meeting this contract.

Similarly, in 1819 John H. Hall began to produce breech-loading rifles with interchangeable parts. By 1825 Hall produced one thousand rifles at his facilities in Harpers Ferry. His weapons, according to Edwin Battison in *Muskets to Mass Production*, "represented the highest degree of precision and interchangeability to date." Over the years many innovations and improvements were introduced which further contributed to the development of an interchangeable system of manufacturing. The idea was becoming an established reality, and in Windsor it finally manifested itself as a complete system. From Windsor this new manufacturing system began to extend to the rest of the world.

That Windsor — and later Springfield — became so important in the development of machine tools and manufacturing methods was surprising. Remote from the larger industrial centers of New England, there was not even a railroad to the area when Robbins and Lawrence first began to manufacture rifles in the 1840s. Any disadvantages in location were compensated, however, by the genius of the men who worked there.

In the 1830s numerous custom gun shops were located in Windsor, including one named N. Kendall & Co. This firm regularly made guns at Windsor prison, using the labor of prisoners for the less fine work. There was nothing unique about this company, and no doubt it would have been forgotten if Richard Lawrence had not appeared.

Lawrence was born in 1817 in Chester, Vermont. When he was two years old, his family moved to the vicinity of Watertown, New York, where he grew up. As a child mechanical devices fascinated him, and he spent much of his time in a nearby gun shop. By age seventeen he was expert in the repair of guns. This expertise found no outlet, however, until he came to Windsor in 1838 to visit friends and relatives. There he offered to repair a rifle for a Doctor Story. When the doctor saw how greatly improved his rifle was, he took Lawrence to N. Kendall & Co., which hired him immediately. Within six months Lawrence had mastered every process in the factory. He was placed in charge of the shop.

In 1842 N. Kendall & Co. gave up the manufacture of guns, and for a time

Lawrence remained as foreman in charge of the prison shop carriage department. Then in 1843 he and Kendall started a custom gun shop. With the addition of a third partner, this company soon expanded and achieved world recognition. Lawrence possessed the mechanical genius to organize the large scale production of rifles, but a new, third partner provided the business acumen. This was S. E. Robbins, a retired lumberman whose business had been in Maine. He approached Kendall and Lawrence with the idea of bidding on a government contract for ten thousand rifles, offering to provide the financial base. After talking the matter over, the three formed a new partnership of Robbins, Kendall & Lawrence.

Many opposed awarding so large a contract to an unknown company, but as the Robbins, Kendall & Lawrence bid was lowest, the contract was granted to them. It specified that they were to manufacture ten thousand rifles at a cost of $10.90 per rifle, and that the work was to be completed within three years. By 1846 the partners had built a new factory in Windsor, where they employed top workers in metalwork and manufacturing, and where they also developed the most advanced manufacturing methods of the time. With their operation fully based on a system of interchangeability, the modern factory had appeared. The ten thousand rifles were delivered eighteen months ahead of time.

Nervous about Robbins' handling of the company's finances, Kendall sold his interest in the firm, which now continued as Robbins & Lawrence. Having so successfully completed the first contract, Robbins & Lawrence were immediately given another order for fifteen thousand rifles. In 1850 they received another contract to make five thousand Jennings

Robbins, Kendall & Lawrence rifle (right), exhibited at the Crystal Palace in London, 1851. Rifle with interchangeable parts (left), made by Robbins & Lawrence after the 1851 Exhibit and before England's Enfield Armory was equipped. Courtesy The American Precision Museum.

rifles. In addition to manufacturing rifles, the company also began to design and build improved manufacturing machinery.

The high point of Robbins & Lawrence was reached in 1851, when they exhibited their rifles at the Crystal Palace industrial exhibition in London. The rifles not only received an award, they attracted so much attention that the British Parliament sent a commission to the United States to study what they named the "American System" of interchangeable manufacturing. The commission was also charged with obtaining the necessary machinery to introduce this system at the Enfield Armory near London. Robbins & Lawrence subsequently received an order from England for twenty-five thousand rifles with interchangeable parts as well as for 141 metalworking machines to equip the Enfield Armory. Other machines were also ordered from the firm. This order made Robbins & Lawrence the world's first major exporter of fine machine tools.

Robbins & Lawrence's quick success was unfortunately followed by an equally quick demise. First weakened financially by an ill-advised experiment in the production of railroad cars, the company was later forced to default on its contract for the Enfield rifles when droughts in Pennsylvania prevented sawmills from delivering gunstocks. In 1856 Robbins & Lawrence went bankrupt during a general industrial depression.

Despite Robbins and Lawrence's failure within ten years, the company's influence continued. The mechanical ingenuity and business enterprise of its partners had firmly established the principles of modern manufacturing based on interchangeability. The machine tool industry also remained prominent in Windsor. In 1860 Robbins & Lawrence was sold and reorganized as Lamson, Goodnow & Yale. In succeeding years the company was reorganized under various names, and in 1889 it (then Jones & Lamson Machine Co.) moved to Springfield, Vermont. There, and in Windsor, the production of machine tools has remained important.

Today, the American Precision Museum in Windsor is located in the original Robbins & Lawrence factory.

The armory and car shops of Robbins & Lawrence in Windsor. Courtesy The American Precision Museum.

Justin Smith Morrill and the Land-Grant Colleges

INDUSTRIAL development, with its new technical and scientific innovations, required better-educated workers. But agriculture, too, was changing in the nineteenth century. Scientific principles were beginning to be applied to farming, in an attempt to increase efficiency and yield. Along with the industrial worker, the farmer needed a better education. In almost every region of the United States — from the Northeast with its growing industries, to the West with its expanding farm settlements — more advanced education was becoming a necessity.

To meet this growing need, numerous schools and colleges were established in the United States in the nineteenth century, and curriculums were revised and expanded. A great many people contributed to this expansion, but one of the most important figures in American education was a man from the Upper Valley. In 1862 Congress enacted the Land Grant Act, authored by Justin Smith Morrill of Strafford, Vermont. This piece of legislation made available thirty thousand acres of federal public lands to each member of Congress. The money received from this land was to be used by each state "to the endowment, support, and maintenance of at least one college where the leading object shall be . . . to teach such branches of learning as are related to agriculture and the mechanic arts. . . ." The Act also stated that "the liberal and practical education of the industrial classes" was to be promoted. Subsequently, the United States established a state system of universities with both altered curriculums and greatly expanded student bodies.

Morrill came to politics relatively late in life. He was born April 14, 1810,

in the village of Strafford, and as a young child he attended the town school. Later he was enrolled in the Thetford Academy, where, as he later wrote, "the preceptor, Mr. Fitch, drilled us in compositions and required accuracy in punctuation as well as in grammar." He wanted to go to college, but his father had three other sons, each of whom he felt should have an equal chance. Unable to send four sons to college, the father sent none, and at age fifteen Morrill left school and began to work.

Morrill's first job was as a clerk for Jedediah Harris in a Strafford general store. After two years he traveled to Portland, Maine, where he worked for another two years in a drygoods business. Returning to Strafford in 1830, he again worked for Harris. In 1834, when he was twenty-four, Harris proposed "to form a partnership in trade under the name of Harris & Morrill." This business flourished, and in 1848 Morrill sold his interest and retired from the partnership.

During the years when Morrill was in business he continued his own education. He read extensively, started a subscription for a town library in 1827, and in 1831 helped found a lyceum. He also participated in local politics and served as director on the boards of various banks. Because of his many activities, he was well known and respected throughout the community. Many viewed him as a perfect political candidate.

Morrill had not thought of entering politics. In 1851 he married Miss Ruth Barrell Swan of Easton, Massachusetts, and assumed he would spend the rest of his life in his newly built home in Strafford. But, as he later wrote: "In 1854,

Thetford Academy. It opened in 1819. Courtesy Baker Library.

when I was forty-four years old, some of my friends came to me to say that I might go to Congress if I desire. I replied that if my county was solid for me I would enter the canvass, but otherwise I would not, as I did not want any struggle. The leaders, at a meeting held at the court-house, agreed to stand by me, and I went to the convention and was nominated with practical unanimity." The election for a seat in the House of Representatives in Washington was not so easy, however. Morrill won with a plurality of only fifty-nine votes.

This narrow victory marked the beginning of an extraordinarily long political career. Subsequently, Morrill served forty-three consecutive years in the House and Senate under twelve different presidents, from Franklin Pierce to William McKinley. Over the years he became one of the most influential politicians in Washington. In the House he was the chairman of the Committee of Ways and Means. In the Senate he chaired the Committee on Finance and the Committee on Public Buildings and Grounds. As chairman of this latter committee, Morrill was especially instrumental in enhancing the physical surroundings of Washington. He

was largely responsible for the Library of Congress and (along with fellow Vermonter George Perkins Marsh) for the completion of the Washington Monument. He had a fine aesthetic sense and contributed greatly to the planning and construction of many of the terraces, fountains, and gardens in the city.

Among Morrill's many contributions as a representative and senator, his Land Grant Act of 1862 stands out. He first introduced this legislation in 1859, but it was vetoed by President Buchanan. Morrill persisted and resubmitted a new bill. In 1862 it was at last passed and signed by President Lincoln. The importance of Morrill's legislation extended well beyond the fact that the individual states were provided with federal lands to be used in the establishment of colleges. The stipulations contained in the Land Grant Act as to who and what were to be taught radically altered American education.

Throughout the first half of the nineteenth century, American colleges were generally modeled after European ones. Most were denominationally inspired and most were reserved for the education of those entering the professions: the ministry, teaching, medicine, law. The

JUSTIN SMITH MORRILL. *Oil on canvas, by Carrie E. Dow Sanborn. Courtesy Vermont Division for Historic Preservation.*

term "higher education" does not really describe these institutions. Students usually entered in their early teens and graduated at an age now considered close to a minimum for college freshmen.

The curriculum was narrow, having remained essentially the same for two hundred years. It adhered strongly to the concepts of the Middle Ages, and a subject was usually not taught unless it was honored by tradition. Philosophy, theology, Latin, ancient Greek, and mathematics constituted the main part of the curriculum. Recalling his Yale experience, Andrew D. White wrote, "The minds of the students were supposed to be developed in the same manner as are the livers of the geese at Strasburg —

every day sundry spoons of the same mixture forced down all throats alike."

Educational reform was introduced slowly in the nineteenth century, primarily as a result of the emergence of science and the subsequent development of industry and vocations. In 1802, for example, West Point Academy was established by Congress, in part as an attempt to provide a more practical curriculum. Engineering, as related to the military, was a dominant focus. In 1812 a department was created at West Point to teach engineering "in all its branches."

The call to teach agriculture at colleges paralleled the call for teaching science. Continual westward expansion created a demand for improved farming techniques to help settle new lands. Simultaneously, there was a desire to stem the depletion of eastern farm lands through continuous farming. The establishment of agricultural colleges was intended to meet these needs.

Despite a widespread desire to establish colleges with more practical curriculums, the many attempts prior to the Civil War were generally unsuccessful. Most of the agricultural schools and colleges founded before the Civil War had disappeared before 1862 for lack of funds. In fact, four-fifths of the American colleges founded before the Civil War had ceased to exist by the mid-twentieth century. After the passage of the Land Grant Act of 1862, few colleges failed for financial reasons.

The Morrill legislation provided the financial base to achieve what had been widely advocated — the establishment of a system of colleges with more practical curriculums. Initially, curriculums at the land-grant colleges emphasized agriculture. In 1909, when industry was more fully widespread, the land-grant association resolved that "the mechanic arts" would include "engineering in all its branches and the sciences related to industries." Both "agriculture and the mechanic arts," as specified in the 1862 act, now became an established part of the curriculums in American colleges.

Morrill continued his support for land-grant colleges after the signing of the 1862 bill. Ten years later he introduced a second bill to provide for their further endowment. This bill was defeated in 1873, but again Morrill persisted. During the next seventeen years he resubmitted a proposal to grant further aid to the colleges eleven times, finally achieving success in 1890. A bill passed that year providing annual federal support to all land-grant colleges.

One measure of the success of these two acts is the number of colleges and universities established in the United States. In 1870 there were 563 institutions of higher learning. By 1910 the number had increased to nearly one thousand, and enrollment totaled one third of a million. Many of these new institutions were land grant colleges, including such present-day state universities as Ver-

mont, New Hampshire, Massachusetts, Iowa, Illinois, and California. In accordance with the Land Grant Act, enrollment had been extended to the nonprofessional classes. In contrast, the sixteen universities of France had at the time an enrollment of about forty thousand students — a number equalled by the faculty members at American institutions.

The tremendous increase in the number of colleges and the number of students enrolled greatly altered the public's idea of college and university. No longer limited to a small minority seeking to enter professions, the curriculums were adapted to fit the practical needs of a new and enlarged student body. Preparation for practical vocations as well as for professions was now part of college education. American higher education had been democratized, and a major force leading to this was the legislation authored by Congressman Justin Smith Morrill.

South porch of the Justin Smith Morrill home in Strafford. From left to right are Senator Morrill, his wife Ruth B. Swan Morrill, their son James, and Mrs. Morrill's sister Louise Swan. Courtesy Vermont Division for Historic Preservation.

135

THE MORRILL MAUSOLEUM

LESS THAN two hundred yards away from the house in which Morrill was born stands the Morrill Mausoleum. Set on the crest of a hill in the Strafford cemetery, the mausoleum was originally visible from each of the three roads which lead into the village. Although not so plainly visible today, it still remains an imposing memorial.

The idea for the mausoleum's construction came when Morrill's wife of forty-seven years, Ruth Barrell Swan Morrill, died in May 1898. Deeply grieved, Morrill made plans for the mausoleum, and work began that summer. Morrill stipulated that all stones come from Vermont quarries, and the exterior stone was Barre granite, cut in the largest available pieces to make a minimum number of joints. The base measures twelve feet by eighteen feet and has a height of twenty feet. All stones except the capstone were prepared at the quarries, then transported by rail to Sharon, where they were drawn to Strafford by horses.

The capstone forms the entire roof of the structure. The first stone, when partially dressed, was rejected when a flaw was discovered. The second stone was flawless. The *Interstate Journal* reported that "its weight in the rough was thirty tons and when completed twenty-two tons. It was beveled on the lower side, thus fitting over and binding together the already immovable walls so that not even a cataclysm can stir it."

The capstone could not be unloaded at the Sharon station, because the highway bridge across the White River was considered unsafe for such a weight. The stone was therefore taken across the railroad bridge about two miles from Sharon. A special carriage was sent from Buffalo, New York, to move the stone. Although twenty-four horses were hitched to the carriage, they were not adequate for the task of moving the stone the ten miles to Strafford. After three days the horses had pulled the stone less than a half mile.

It was decided then to move the stone by capstan. The road before the stone was planked, pulleys were fastened to trees, and a pair of horses were used for the necessary force. After moving the capstone about four miles work had to be stopped. It was late November, and the cold weather and frozen ground made the possibility of an accident too great. The stone was moved from the road and covered with boards to await the coming spring.

Because of the delay in moving the capstone, Morrill never saw the completion of the mausoleum. In mid-December 1898 he fell ill with a cold in Washington. The cold progressed into pneumonia, and he died on December 28, 1898.

In the late spring of 1899 work on the transportation of the capstone began again. Progress was slow, and it was not until July 11 that the stone was at last swung into place by straining derricks. "A few days later," the *Interstate Journal* reported, "there was committed to its keeping all that was mortal of Senator Morrill and his wife."

Courtesy Baker Library.

The Tilden Female Seminary

FEMALE education was not common in the first half of the nineteenth century. Nevertheless, the Upper Valley provided some educational opportunites for girls. A girls' school, run by Catherine Fiske, operated in Keene, New Hampshire, from 1814 to 1837, and in Hanover a series of female academies were located in private homes. The largest and longest-lasting of these was established by Mrs. Maria B. Peabody in 1840.

In the 1830s educational opportunities for girls began to expand in the United States when numerous female seminaries were established. The word "seminary" was used to mean school or academy and was often applied to girls' schools. Over the next thirty years an increasing number of girls' schools were built, and by 1860 girls' schools existed in almost every state. Toward the end of this period of expansion, the Tilden Female Seminary was built in West Lebanon.

The Tilden Female Seminary differed from most of the earlier schools for girls in the Upper Valley in that it was not an individual undertaking within a private home. The school was chartered by the legislature of New Hampshire, and instruction was provided in a school building perched above the Connecticut River in West Lebanon. The founding of the school came largely at the wishes of one man, William Tilden. A native of West Lebanon, Tilden had moved to New York, where he had become wealthy through the manufacture and export of

School portrait of the Tilden Female Seminary, about 1880.
Hiram Orcutt probably stands at the rear. Courtesy Baker Library.

varnish. Wanting to give something to his hometown, Tilden contributed ten of the fifteen thousand dollars needed to build and open the school. Later he also paid for its expansion.

The school was dedicated on September 19, 1855. No record exists to tell how many young girls attended the Tilden Female Seminary the first year, but the original prospectus stated that fifty places were available — forty for boarders and ten for day students. The prospectus also stressed that the school had ''a bathing room, accessible to all boarders, conveniently fitted up for cold, warm, and shower baths.''

The course of study at Tilden Female Seminary lasted three years and was divided into Junior, Middle, and Senior classes. There was also a ''Preparatory Department, for such as are not qualified to join the Junior Class.'' When the school first opened, instruction was year-round, with several short vacations interspersed throughout. Later this was changed, and a twelve-week summer vacation was introduced to reduce travel costs and to avoid instruction during the hot weather.

The goals of early girls' schools were generally ''to prepare for life,'' rather than for college or for a profession. The assumption was that a woman's chief occupation was homemaking. Consequently, early curriculums stressed domestic training and religious and moral education. When, later in the nineteenth century, more and more women entered occupations outside the household, especially nursing and teaching, curriculums at the female seminaries were altered to provide a more substantial and intellectual course of study. The results, however, were not always the best. Many girls' schools simply introduced a course of study found in boys' academies, without questioning whether such a curriculum was good for either boys or girls. Another major criticism leveled at female seminaries was that they tried to teach too many subjects, ranging from the arts to science, yet failed to teach thoroughly any single one.

The actual content of the courses taught at the Tilden Female Seminary is not known. An examination of its course offerings, however, indicates that this seminary, like many others of the time, prided itself on its highly diverse curriculum. French, Latin, English grammar and composition were taught, as were algebra, natural philosophy, logic, and rhetoric. There was also a strong emphasis on science. Botany and astronomy were taken in the junior year and zoology in the middle year. In the senior year there was a course on political economy. There were a few courses in religion as well, and music and the ''ornamental branches'' were not forgotten. As was written in a later prospectus, without these ''no system of female education would be complete.''

Like many girls' schools in the nineteenth century, the Tilden Female Seminary attracted girls from towns near and far. In fact, many of those attending the Tilden Seminary came from outside New England. When the school first opened, many women from the South traveled northward to West Lebanon for their schooling. The Civil War disrupted this pattern, causing enrollment to decline. The school suffered further under its third principal, L. H. Deane, who was so bad that enrollment dropped to a handful of women. Deane resigned in October 1864, and the school closed until the following spring, when Hiram Orcutt became the new principal.

Under Hiram Orcutt the Tilden Female Seminary blossomed into a thriving New England institution for women. Women attended from the South and the Midwest and a few from as far away as California. After enrollment climbed quickly to seventy-five, it was decided to enlarge the building. In 1868, two wings were added to the school. That same year the school's name was officially changed to Tilden Seminary, though many continued to refer to it as the Tilden Female Seminary or Tilden Ladies Seminary.

Despite various changes under Orcutt, the course of study remained essentially the same. A typical day was described in a letter written in 1869 by one of the students. At 7:30 A.M. the chapel bell rang, and the students dressed and answered to their names. They then filed out two by two and walked for about twenty minutes in whatever direction Mrs. Orcutt led them. The study bell rang at 8:00, and there was a study period until 8:45. This was followed by prayer in the chapel. On the day described in the letter there was a history class in the morning. Another morning class was elocution, held in the gymnasium. Dinner was at 1:00 P.M., followed by a literature class at 2:00. At 4:00 were prayers, then tea at 5:15. Gymnastics were held at 6:00, and there was study period from 7:30 to 9:00. At 10:00 everyone went to bed. Breakfast and supper were not mentioned in the letter, and no document exists which mentions when they might have been.

It was a long day, regulated at all times. No visits with "intimate acquaintances" outside the school were allowed, unless a student had the written consent of parent or guardian. This rule was apparently broken often, as many of the girls from the Tilden Seminary did have contact with male students from Dartmouth. Despite the regimentation, there seems to have been few complaints. The same letter which described the school day complained only of the coffee and the facilities for washing clothes.

Orcutt served as principal of the school until 1880. After his departure enrollment began to decline, and in 1890 the school closed permanently. The reasons why the Tilden Seminary closed when it did are uncertain. No doubt Orcutt's personality was itself a sustaining force. When he left, the school lost an important attribute. But there were other factors as well. At the end of the century education for women was no longer new, and public high schools were offering what previously had been obtainable only in seminaries and academies. The Tilden Seminary could no longer rely on its uniqueness as a school for girls to attract pupils. Consequently, the seminary, like most other female seminaries in the country, closed its doors.

Today, West Lebanon's junior high school stands where the Tilden Seminary once stood, and the hill overlooking the Connecticut is still called Seminary Hill.

Toward a New Era

THE 1880s TO THE

EARLY TWENTIETH CENTURY

The Rise of the Dairy Industry

Dairy farming is prevalent today in the Upper Valley and other parts of the hill country. Larger farms with cleared grazing land generally have milk cows; tanker trucks filled with milk are a common sight on the roads. For most of the twentieth century dairying has been a dominant industry in the region, and most likely that situation will continue in the foreseeable future.

Despite dairy farming's importance for the region during this century, it was reluctantly adopted by farmers. In fact, the shift to dairying came only when there was practically no alternative. In the second half of the nineteenth century, agriculture in Vermont and New Hampshire underwent a dramatic transformation. Unable to compete with western markets, the production of staple crops plummeted. Wheat production, for example, almost vanished, dropping over 90 percent in both states between 1849 and 1899. During the same period corn production decreased over 30 percent. Even sheep farming, once so dominant, was in rapid decline.

The farmers' reluctance to take up dairying is easy to understand. As Harold Wilson aptly pointed out in *The Hill Country of Northern New England*, "The care of cows was a much less attractive task than the herding of sheep. Milking was a tedious job. . . . The cows must be milked twice a day, and the milk taken care of at once. The dairy farmer had to begin work as early on Sundays as on other days, and if he went away from the farm in the afternoon, he had to be back in time to 'get the cows in' and milk them. The man who raised sheep had no such chores. Indeed, during the summer season sheep required little more attention than to be salted once or twice a week."

Until the 1850s dairy farming was completely private in Vermont and New Hampshire. Butter and cheese were made by the individual farmer, and cream was obtained by placing milk in shallow pans and skimming off the top. Almost no milk was produced during the late autumn and winter months, when cows were let go dry. Those with larger herds took their surplus themselves to sell in city markets, while those with only a few cows sold to local merchants, frequently accepting goods in return for payment.

Making cheese and butter was a laborious process. When, in increasing numbers, northern New England farmers began to shift to dairying, they sought ways to minimize labor and to improve efficiency. A major innovation was the introduction of associated dairying, which involved the manufacture of cheese or butter in a centrally situated factory. First introduced in New York in 1851, the associated dairying system quickly spread to northern New England. In 1854 the first cheese factory in Vermont was established in the town of Wells, and by 1900 sixty-six cheese factories had been built in Vermont.

The introduction of the factory as an integral and essential part of farming signified a dramatic change. Farming was no longer necessarily separate from industry, but could be integrated with it. In ensuing years the integration of farming with industry greatly increased.

Initially popular, cheese factories soon lost significance in the hill country. Competition from the Midwestern and Western states began once more to undermine the area's position. Increased cheese production in the West resulted in a drop in Vermont's output from a high of 5,582,327 pounds in 1889 to 4,713,105 pounds in 1899. Ten years later Vermont's cheese production had dropped another 2,000,000 pounds.

The decrease in cheese production did not dampen the growth of the area's dairy industry. Instead of cheese, farmers began to produce butter in ever-increasing quantities. Through the end of the nineteenth century, considerable quantities of butter were produced privately on the farms. In 1899, for example, almost 8,000,000 pounds of butter were made on New Hampshire farms, and in Vermont, over 23,000,000 pounds.

Even more butter was being made in creameries. The making of butter in a factory meant less labor for the overworked farmwives and insured a uniformity of quality and freshness. In the 1880s creameries were built throughout northern New England, resulting in enormous increases in butter production. In New Hampshire only 100,000 pounds of butter were made in factories in 1879. Ten years later, the total had jumped to 2,000,000 pounds. And by 1899, 5,000,000 pounds of butter were produced in fifty-three creameries throughout New Hampshire. In Vermont the increases were even more dramatic. Between 1879 and 1899 the amount of butter produced in factories soared from 5,000 pounds to 22,000,000. That year there were 189 creameries in Vermont —

more than three times the number in New Hampshire.

In the years before 1900, the dairy industry continued to grow in Vermont and New Hampshire, and as it grew a variety of improvements were introduced. Better and more efficient ways of caring for the cows were developed. Winter dairying also became more common. Technical improvements were also introduced, including the centrifugal separator and the "Babcock Tester," used to measure the quantity of butterfat in milk. By 1900 the dairy industry was the leading industry in Vermont, with half of the state's farms primarily dairy farms. In New Hampshire a third of the farms were primarily dairy.

The year 1899 marked the height of butter production in the two states. Ten years later butter production in Vermont had fallen from a high of 46 million to 35 million pounds, and by 1919 it had plummeted to 17 million. The output of butter in New Hampshire declined just as precipitously over the same twenty years. By 1919 its butter production had dropped to 5 million pounds.

The rapid decline of butter production in the northern New England hill country was the result of increased but-

A typical late nineteenth century Vermont farm milking scene. Courtesy Vermont Historical Society.

Sanatoga Springs. Note the many small trees planted to give the appearance of a park. Courtesy Woodstock Historical Society.

Sheldon, Vergennes, Williamstown, and Brunswick Springs.

One of Vermont's most famous spas was at Clarendon. People traveled from as far away as Virginia and the Carolinas to drink its waters. Clarendon Springs' reputation was enhanced by the belief that its waters aided human fertility. W. Storrs Lee recounts in *The Green Mountains of Vermont* how a local census had revealed that eight families living in Clarendon had produced 113 children. None of the eight husbands had more than one wife, and only one set of twins was among the 113 children. For many, this statistic was proof enough that the Clarendon waters increased fertility.

Lacking the springs believed crucial for a resort, Woodstock discovered — or rather, rediscovered — a "famous" source of mineral waters. In the early 1800s bubbling waters had been discovered in Woodstock at a place called Sanderson's Spring. People came to seek cures for kidney troubles, dyspepsia, scrofula, and other ailments, but they soon lost their belief in the spring's curative powers and the waters were forgotten.

In 1850 the waters at Sanderson's Spring were analyzed, and the scientific proof that they contained a variety of chemicals was enough to attract the halt and the lame back to Woodstock in

tion. The "something else" came in the form of invention. First, Sanderson's Spring was rechristened Sanatoga Springs — as close a plagarism of nearby Saratoga Springs as possible. Next, the qualities of the waters were dressed up with "expert" testimony. An early brochure asserted, "From the fact that the water of the Sanatoga Springs maintains such an even temperature throughout the year, it is claimed by experts that it comes from a great depth, percolating through many formations of strata, thus rendering it exceptionally pure and free from organic matter."

Perhaps remembering that the water at Sanderson's Spring had never been successful in cures, the promoters did not overemphasize the curative powers of Sanatoga Springs. Claimed cures were generally minor ones. "In cases of ivy poison," the promotional literature stated, "the soothing effects are almost miraculous. . . . For divers poisons, for inflammation and skin diseases it has proved a patent remedy." The brochures praised the digestibility of the water. "One fact worthy of notice is the quantity of Sanatoga which can be taken without experiencing any sense of fullness or discomfort. One patient drank twelve glasses within thirty minutes at the Spring and afterwards continued its use at the rate of twelve glasses a day with the greatest benefit in a severe case of scrofula."

The rebirth of Sanderson's Spring as Sanatoga Springs provided investors with the confidence necessary to build a hotel. In 1892 the Woodstock Inn opened, complimented by a newly developed fifteen-acre park around the new springhouse of Sanatoga Springs. A brochure described the park as terraced, with "rustic bridges. . . . Five hundred trees have been set out, two hundred feet of stairway built leading to a Pavilion at the summit of the Park, which is also reached by a bridle path."

With the building of the Woodstock Inn, Woodstock quickly became a popular resort for the wealthy. "Its riotous winter parties were the talk of Boston and Mon-

Vermont Historical Society

search of miraculous cures. Sanderson's Spring did not provide many cures, however, and for a second time Woodstock's medicinal waters were forgotten. No doubt they would have remained forgotten, but in 1890 Woodstock needed a mineral springs if the town were to be developed into a resort. Once more Sanderson's Spring was rediscovered.

But more than the rediscovery of Sanderson's Spring was needed to attract investors and to insure the success of a resort hotel in Woodstock. The waters had never worked before, so the promoters could not use their past history as a selling point. Something else was necessary to make the spring an attrac-

149

ISLAND HOUSE
BELLOWS FALLS, Vᵗ.

R. SHURTLEFF, Proprietor.

DISTANCES
from Bellows Falls.

SOUTH.

Westminster,	4
Putney,	15
Dummerston,	19
Brattleboro',	24
Vernon,	29
South Vernon,	34
Bernardston,	41
Greenfield,	48
Deerfield,	51
South Deerfield,	56
Whately,	58
Hatfield,	63
Northampton,	67
Smith's Ferry,	71
Holyoke,	73
Willimansett,	74
Cabotville,	80
Springfield,	85
Longmeadow,	87
Thompsonville,	92
Warehouse Point,	96
Windsor Locks,	98
Windsor,	103
Hartford,	110
New Britain,	119
Berlin,	121
Meriden,	128
Wallingford,	133
North Haven,	133
New Haven,	148
Milford,	156
Stratford,	160
Bridgeport,	164
Fairfield,	168
Southport,	170
Westport,	175
Norwalk,	178
Darien,	181
Stamford,	186
Greenwich,	191
Port Chester,	194
Rye Station,	196
Marmarick,	199
New Rochelle,	203
Williams Bridge,	209
32d Street,	220
Canal St. in New York,	222

Passenger Trains leave

Bellows Falls for Brattleboro', Greenfield, Springfield, Hartford, New Haven, and N. York, 9.00 A. M., 2.40 P. M.

Keene, Fitchburg, Worcester, Lowell and Boston, 8.58 A. M., 2.00 and 3.15 P. M.

Whitehall & Saratoga Sp'gs, 11.45 A. M.

Albany, 8.45 A. M.

BILL OF FARE.

MONDAY, DECEMBER 15, 1851.

SOUP.
Rice.

BOILED.	**ROAST.**
Pork and Cabbage.	Beef.
Corned Beef.	Turkey, Giblet Sauce.
Ham.	Chicken, Cranberry Sauce.
Chicken and Pork.	Pork.
Tongue.	Goose, Apple Sauce.

SIDE DISHES.
Stewed Mutton with Potatoes.
Stewed Chicken on Toast.
Fried Pork and Potatoes.
Rice Croquetts.
Apple Fritters.

VEGETABLES.

Potatoes Boiled.	Parsnips.
Potatoes Mashed.	Onions.
Pickled Cucumbers.	Beets.
Turnips.	Carrots.
Kole Slaw.	Squash.

PASTRY.

Rice Pudding.	Pumpkin Pies.
Cranberry Tarts.	Apple Pies.
Mince Pies.	Squash Pies.
Custard Pies.	

DESSERT.

Charlotte de Ruse.	Walnuts.
Wine Jelly.	Apples.
Blanc Mange.	Raisins.
Boiled Custards.	Almonds.

DISTANCES
from Bellows Falls.

NORTH.

Rutland & Burlington R. R.

Rockingham,	6
Bartonsville,	10
Chester,	14
Duttonsville,	23
Proctorsville,	25
Ludlow,	28
Mount Holly,	35
Cuttingsville,	42
Rutland,	53
Pittsford,	61
Brandon,	70
Middlebury,	87
Vergennes,	98
Burlington,	118
Ogdensburgh,	280
Montreal,	217
Quebec,	397
Whitehall,	78
Saratoga Springs,	120

Sullivan and Central R. R.

Charlestown,	7
Claremont,	16
Windsor,	25
White River Junction,	40
By Passumpsic R. Road to Wells River,	80
St. Johnsbury,	101
Montpelier, via Vt. Central,	103
Burlington,	141

EAST.

Walpole,	4
Westmoreland,	12
Keene,	22
Marlborough,	28
Troy,	32
Fitzwilliam,	37
State Line,	43
Winchendon,	46
North Ashburnham,	50
South "	54
Westminster,	59
Fitchburg,	64
Groton Junction,	79
Concord,	94
Boston,	114

Passenger Trains leave

Bellows Falls for Rutland, Burlington, Ogdensburgh, Montreal, and Quebec, 11.45 A. M., and 5.20 P. M.

Windsor, White River Junction, St. Johnsbury, Wells River and White Mountains, 11.45 A. M., and 5.20 P. M.

Courtesy Vermont Historical Society.

treal sportsmen," wrote W. Storrs Lee. Sanatoga Springs served also as an attraction to the area, drawing people to its waters. But the life of Sanatoga Springs was short. By the beginning of the twentieth century people sought cures for their ailments at the drugstore and in the hospital, rather than at some unpleasant-tasting spring. As had happened twice before, the waters at Sanatoga Springs were soon forgotten. Woodstock, however, continued to grow as a resort area, despite the demise of its invented springs. The notion that vacations must be bound to springs or other curative waters had finally passed.

ROBERTSON'S SPRING AT BELLOWS FALLS

THE DESIRE to find a cure in any foul-tasting water led at times to unpleasant extremes, as in the case of Robertson's Spring in Bellows Falls. Two miles south of Bellows Falls, at Walpole, are located the Abenaqui Springs. These springs, originally used by the Indians, had little attraction for European settlers until 1851, when the proprietor of the Island House in Bellows Falls decided mineral waters might increase his business. Bath houses and shower baths were built at the Abenaqui Springs, as well as a large dance pavilion. Coaches ran every two hours between the Island House and the springs, and within a short time the hotel was considered a fashionable place to vacation.

At the same time that the Abenaqui Springs became renowned, a man named Robertson discovered in Bellows Falls yet another spring. Robertson had built a tavern in town and had dug a well for water. After some years a strange taste and smell became evident in the water, and Robertson was convinced he had located a second Abenaqui Springs. Others were equally convinced, and within a short time people began to travel long distances to seek cures at Robertson's Spring. A great many paid a fee to drink the water and to transport it home; others stayed in the tavern to take the water daily.

In time Robertson decided to clean his well and to improve it. Emptying the well, he found at the bottom the decaying bodies of two cats. That was the end of Robertson's Spring.

House of Dixi Crosby, professor of surgery at Dartmouth from 1840 to 1870. The house still stands, largely unaltered, in Hanover. Courtesy Mary Hitchcock Memorial Hospital.

Mary Hitchcock Memorial Hospital

ON MAY 18, 1893, a thirteen-year-old girl from West Lebanon was admitted to Mary Hitchcock Memorial Hospital. On admission it was noted she had a "hip joint disease," and she was placed under the care of Dr. William T. Smith. A period of observation followed, and then an operation was performed. The girl recovered slowly, and on August 8 she was discharged with her condition noted as "improved."

This was case No. 1 in the hospital records. In the more than ninety years since then, over three hundred thousand people have been admitted to Mary Hitchcock Hospital, and the hospital has expanded into one of the largest institutions in northern New England. The very size of Hitchcock Hospital is a testament to its importance within the community.

Today scarcely anyone in the United States can imagine living in an area without hospital facilities. But that has not always been the case. Before 1900 few small rural towns like Hanover had a hospital. The lack of a hospital was not considered a shortcoming. When hospitals were widely built throughout the United States for the first time in the 1880s and 1890s, most people questioned the necessity of such institutions. The prevalent sentiment was that hospitals cost a great deal to build, yet added little to the medical care already available. In fact, the opening of Hitchcock Hospital was greeted with considerable skepticism. Its thirty-six beds were viewed by many as extravagant and much too large for any demands that would ever be placed upon it.

Until the nineteenth century hospitals generally had negative reputations. In Europe in the seventeenth and eighteenth centuries, hospitals often housed the poor and the insane along with the sick. Sanitary conditions in those institutions were practically nonexistent. Only in the mid-eighteenth century did Europeans begin to separate the curable sick, the insane, and the contagious, but not many improvements were made in regard to cleanliness. In America few hospitals were built before the nineteenth century. Most frequently the patient simply remained at home or was housed at the residence of the physician — which had the medical advantage that the institutional filth of most European hospitals was avoided.

Following the American Revolution, there were nine hospitals in the country, and by 1861 there were sixty-eight. After the Civil War large numbers of hospitals began to be built. The situation in the Upper Valley paralleled the larger pattern prevalent throughout the country. In 1776 one hospital was located in the "Lebanon woods" at a considerable distance from the village. The following year the college mill on Mink Brook — located just below the bridge on the Lebanon road — was converted into a second hospital. Both, however, were isolation centers rather than hospitals in a modern sense. Such hospitals were referred to as "pest houses," and they functioned primarily as places where inoculation against small pox could take place apart from the community at large. The fear that these two hospitals might serve as centers of contagion led to bitter quarrels among the citizens of the area, and both were eventually closed. Many years later Dr. Dixi Crosby of Hanover established a small

Mary Hitchcock Memorial Hospital, about 1903. Taken from Bartlett Tower; Occom Ridge is in the background. Courtesy Mary Hitchcock Memorial Hospital.

The operating theater, about 1895. Courtesy Mary Hitchcock Memorial Hospital.

hospital for the use of his own patients and those of other physicians connected with the Dartmouth Medical School. Its location was the house on College Street north of the present site of the White Church. This hospital closed when Crosby retired in 1870.

The resident staff of the Dartmouth Medical School felt keenly the lack of hospital facilities. To encourage the building of a hospital, they helped organize the Dartmouth Medical Association in 1885. Over a period of five years the Association acquired some land and raised a small amount of money for the building. It was Hiram Hitchcock's donation, however, that made the hospital possible.

In 1889 Hitchcock announced his intention to build at his own expense a hospital suitable for the Hanover region.

The hospital was also to serve the needs of the Dartmouth Medical School. To implement this gift a charter was obtained in August 1889 from the New Hampshire legislature. Construction began shortly after and continued for three years. On May 3, 1893, the completed hospital was dedicated.

No one knows exactly what Hitchcock spent for construction of the hospital. All bills submitted were simply paid, and no accounting was made to anyone. Little seems to have been spared in the way of expense. Early Italian Renaissance was selected as the style of architecture, and the hospital was one of the first built in America on a pavilion plan. Located in the center was "a large hall, with marble mosaic floors, walls finished in quartered oak and marble, ornamented by pillars, and containing a

The women's ward, about 1900 (above). The ward was heated by a central fireplace which can be seen today in the employees' lounge. A private room (left). Note the absence of institutional furniture. Courtesy Mary Hitchcock Memorial Hospital.

155

finely designed fireplace of Siena marble." (The hall has been preserved, undisturbed by newer construction.) In addition to patients' rooms, waiting rooms, dining rooms, kitchen, and laundry, there was a large surgical unit containing a high, domed operating theater. This was lighted by a large skylight and seated 150 persons.

Initially, community reaction to the hospital was somewhat negative. Even some professors in the Dartmouth Medical School were surprised at the size of the completed hospital. They had imagined a small cottage hospital, much like that of Dr. Crosby, to be suitable for their purposes. As was true in the country as a whole, many valley residents considered the hospital a white elephant which the town could never utilize or support. A hospital, they believed, served only as a refuge for the poor or a place for drastic surgery. Ordinary illnesses, no matter how serious, were to be treated in the home, and many people were opposed to replacing the home environment with an institutional one. Another prevalent attitude was that a baby delivered in a hospital rather than in the parents' home was somehow not properly born.

Nationally, these attitudes gradually changed, as hospitals became integral parts of their communities. In the Upper Valley, too, all skepticism quickly vanished, and the Hitchcock Hospital became firmly established. In 1900, only seven years after the hospital had opened, Hiram Hitchcock died, leaving no endowment for continued operations. Nevertheless, the hospital was by then able to support itself. By 1900 the average daily occupancy at Hitchcock Hospital was already 15.2. In 1905 average occupancy had increased to 28.7, and by 1913 it was 40.7 — exceeding the thirty-six beds originally considered so extravagant.

Community acceptance of the hospital was rapid, but some old attitudes were slow to change. For several years many still viewed the hospital as a place primarily for surgery. In 1915-1916 surgical cases constituted 72 percent of all cases at Hitchcock Hospital. Slowly this changed, and by 1925 surgical cases comprised only 55 percent of all cases, while 45 percent were medical and obstetrical. In the same year 115 babies were born at the hospital. By then Hitchcock Hospital was viewed by the community as a proper place for medical treatment.

THE MARY HITCHCOCK SCHOOL OF NURSING

HIRAM HITCHCOCK wanted the Mary Hitchcock Memorial Hospital to include a program for the training of nurses, so when the hospital opened, the Training School for Nurses was also established. The first class had two students, and the course of study was two years.

The founding of a school for nurses at Hitchcock Hospital followed a trend throughout the United States. Prior to the end of the nineteenth century, nursing was looked upon with considerable suspicion. Nursing generally represented the lowest work, and the moral character of a nurse often stood in question. In some city hospitals, nursing duties were performed by elderly female jail inmates. Conditions in most hospitals were deplorable, and nurses were usually women who could find no other work.

This situation continued unchanged until the Civil War, when a call went out for nurses to aid the wounded and dying. Hundreds of women volunteered, and during the war more than two thousand women from the North and South served as nurses. At the war's conclusion nursing quickly developed as a respected profession. In 1873 the first three American nursing schools, based on a plan developed by Florence Nightingale, were established. Ten years later there were twenty-two nursing schools in the country, and by the end of the century the number had multiplied tenfold.

The nursing school at Hitchcock Hospital was founded during this expansion. The first two students arrived in July 1893; others were admitted as vacancies occurred. Admission required the applicant be female, between the ages of twenty-one and thirty-five, strong, healthy, and of good common sense. After a two-month probationary period a student became a junior or first-year nurse. In exchange for services to the hospital, she received her training.

All students worked six and one-half days. New students worked day duty from 7:00 A.M. to 8:00 P.M., with time off for meals and a two-hour break sometime during the day. After three months they were included in the night schedule, from 8:00 P.M. to 7:00 A.M. During the first years, when the hospital's occupancy rate was low, student nurses also worked in private homes in Hanover and surrounding towns. A small pamphlet given to families and patients explained the duties of the nurse in the home. Room and board were to be provided, plus payment of $1.00 per day for junior nurses and $1.50 for seniors. First-year nurses were to be given time off to attend one-hour classes five days a week. The brochure also stated that the nurse "must not be expected to share the patient's bed."

The nursing school expanded rapidly in its early years, and by 1903 there were twenty-one students. The school continued in existence until 1980, when the last class was graduated. That year Hitchcock's nursing school was replaced by a new program operated in affiliation with Colby-Sawyer College in New London, New Hampshire. The new program provides nurses with a Bachelor of Science degree.

Nursing Students, 1903. Courtesy Mary Hitchcock Memorial Hospital.

Mary and Hiram Hitchcock, about 1865. Courtesy Baker Library.

MARY AND HIRAM HITCHCOCK

TWO YEARS after Mary Hitchcock died in 1887, her husband Hiram resolved to build a hospital in Hanover as a fitting memorial to her memory. Only a few facts are known about the person Mary Hitchcock, neé Maynard. She was born in 1834 in Drewsville, New Hampshire, where she was also raised. After a long courtship, she married Hiram Hitchcock in 1858, and in the course of their marriage she gave birth to two children who died as infants. At one point Hiram presented her with a copy of the Crown Jewels of Russia. She died at age 53.

Hiram Hitchcock was born in Claremont, New Hampshire, on August 27, 1832. When he was ten years old, his family moved to Drewsville. Later, he traveled to New Orleans where he began work at the St. Charles Hotel. He rose rapidly in the hotel profession, working several years in New Orleans and later in Nahant, Massachusetts. Following his marriage to Mary, he moved to New York City, where he established with two others the Fifth Avenue Hotel.

In 1866 Hiram retired from active participation in the management of the hotel because of ill health, and he and his wife embarked on a variety of travels. In 1870 the Hitchcocks moved to Hanover, where they lived in a house with extensive grounds reaching to the Connecticut River — now the site of the newer Dartmouth dormitories, the Tuck and Thayer schools, and Tuck Drive. Hanover remained the Hitchcocks' principal residence even after 1879, when Hiram resumed an active share in the management of the Fifth Avenue Hotel.

While in Hanover, Hiram served as a representative to the State Legislature, was president of Dartmouth National and Dartmouth Savings Bank, and a trustee of the New Hampshire College of Agriculture and the Mechanic Arts (now the University of New Hampshire). From 1878 to 1892 he was also a trustee of Dartmouth College. In addition to building Mary Hitchcock Hospital, Hiram made other contributions to Dartmouth and the town of Hanover. In 1889, for example, he provided most of the funds for remodeling the college church. He was unable to provide an endowment for the Hitchcock Hospital because his fortune was depleted in the early 1890s by a failed project to build a canal across Nicaragua. In 1900, seven years after the completion of Hitchcock Hospital, Hiram died of pneumonia.

Saint-Gaudens Comes to Cornish

IN 1885 the sculptor Augustus Saint-Gaudens traveled for the first time to Cornish, New Hampshire. Arriving in April, he was dismayed at what he saw. It was a dark, rainy day, and the house he intended to rent "appeared so forbidding and relentless that one might have imagined a skeleton half-hanging out of the window, shrieking and dangling in the gale, with the sound of clanking bones." Saint-Gaudens was ready to leave immediately. "I was for fleeing at once and returning to my beloved sidewalks of New York," he wrote in his *Reminiscences*. His wife felt otherwise and finally convinced him that they should rent the house for the summer.

Returning in the summer, Saint-Gaudens fell in love with Cornish, and he decided to make the village his permanent summer residence. He was not alone in his decision. Several artist friends traveled northward to the Upper Valley to visit, and many, struck by the beauty of Mt. Ascutney and the surrounding countryside, decided to purchase summer homes in the town. The painters George DeForest Brush, Thomas W. Dewing, and Henry Oliver Walker were the first to follow Saint-Gaudens to Cornish. Other painters, sculptors, and writers followed — including Charles Platt, the novelist Winston Churchill, Herbert Adams, and Maxfield Parrish — and within a few years Cornish was known as an active artist colony. It was the greatest flowering of the arts the Upper Valley has ever seen.

In part, chance brought Saint-Gaudens to Cornish, and yet it was not completely chance. In 1883 Saint-Gaudens was invited to Chicago to discuss the possibility of creating an Abraham Lincoln monument for one of the city's parks. He agreed to go, wanting more than anything else to do this statue. The talks in Chicago were inconclusive, however, and it was suggested Saint-Gaudens enter a competition to determine who should receive the commission. Saint-Gaudens refused on principle, believing competitions were not properly arranged. No doubt he also remembered with some bitterness his failure several years earlier to win a competition for a statue of Charles Sumner in Boston. Almost a year had passed after Saint-Gaudens' refusal to enter a competition, when in August 1884 the Lincoln statue committee decided to award the commission to him outright. Saint-Gaudens readily accepted and soon began making preparations for the work.

When Saint-Gaudens accepted the commission, he had a studio in New York City, where he was generally content to be. But in April 1885 his wife Augusta began to discuss where they might spend the summer to avoid the New York heat. The small town of Cornish was suggested. "We hit upon Cornish," Saint-Gaudens later wrote, "because, while casting about for a summer residence, Mr. C. C. Beaman [a friend] told me that if I would go up there with him, he had an old house which he would sell me for what he had paid for it, five hundred dollars."

Saint-Gaudens was reluctant to purchase the house, and after the rainy visit in April he was not even certain he wanted to rent it. Upon his return to New York, however, something he had observed in New Hampshire began to change his mind. To persuade Saint-Gaudens to travel to Cornish in the first place, his friend Beaman had promised that there were "plenty of Lincoln-shaped men up there." Saint-Gaudens found this to be true, and back in New York he began to think that completing his model of Lincoln in Cornish might be a good idea after all.

160

Work on the monument for Chicago was Saint-Gaudens' principal concern during his first summer in Cornish. He made a sketch of a standing Lincoln, and then, to complete the model, he employed a Mr. Langdon Morse of Windsor, Vermont, to pose for him. Morse was said to be a "Lincoln-shaped man," standing 6'4" — the same height as Lincoln.

At the end of summer Saint-Gaudens decided he would like to purchase the house he had rented, but Beaman had changed his mind about selling. Beaman said he wanted the house for his children when they were older, but he agreed to rent the house almost indefinitely. Improvements, however, were to be at Saint-Gaudens' own expense. Six years later, when Saint-Gaudens threatened to leave Cornish, Beaman finally agreed to sell the house.

In 1887 Saint-Gaudens completed work on his standing Lincoln, and the statue was cast in bronze by the Henry Bonnard Bronze Company in New York. The statue was shipped to Chicago and placed in Lincoln Park, where on October 22, 1887, it was unveiled with Lincoln's fifteen-year-old grandson removing the flag that draped the tall figure. Critics immediately hailed it as "the greatest portrait statue in the United States." The statue depicts Lincoln in a strikingly realistic manner. Tall, gaunt, and meditative, he appears to have just risen from a chair and to be about to speak. The statue was widely popular and so highly regarded that in 1920 a replica was given to the British to celebrate one hundred years of peace between the two countries. Other replicas, smaller in size, were also made.

In many respects Saint-Gaudens' standing Lincoln is typical of both his own mature work and much of the American sculpture produced at the end of the nineteenth century. In the years following the Civil War the United States underwent a major transformation, as it continued its westward expansion and rapidly developed as an industrial country. An unparalleled economic growth accompanied the industrial development, and the increased wealth brought with it an increased interest in art. In particular, there was widespread interest in public

The first summer in Cornish, 1885. From left to right are Augustus' younger brother Louis, Frederick MacMonnies, Homer, Augusta, and Augustus. Courtesy Saint-Gaudens National Historic Site.

161

Saint-Gaudens, standing beside his recently completed statue of Lincoln, 1887. Courtesy Baker Library.

art, such as sculpture. Municipal art societies sprang up in city after city, each concerned with the erection and ornamentation of public buildings, monuments, and parks. Corporations also began to place sculpture in their buildings. Such societies and corporations were not interested in patronizing just any type of art. They demanded works symbolizing what was perceived as the American experience. The United States had developed into a rich and powerful country; it now desired works of art to give expression to that fact.

Numerous memorial parks were laid out in cities, such as Lincoln Park in Chicago, and appropriate bronze statues were often cast and placed in such parks. Most frequently these statues portrayed their subjects in rugged, naturalistic ways to capture what was widely viewed as American. The naturalism was usually tempered by some idealistic pose, as is the case with Saint-Gaudens' standing Lincoln.

Saint-Gaudens, one of the first American sculptors to create such an art, was one of America's best sculptors of public monuments and memorials. Yet the expression Saint-Gaudens gave to the American experience in the latter part of the nineteenth century was not initially evident in his early work. In fact, his first major work, a statue of Hiawatha, reflected more the aesthetic traditions of Europe than anything American. It is doubtful Saint-Gaudens ever saw an American Indian, and his statue — modeled in Rome — is more a romantic idealization than a realistic portrayal.

Saint-Gaudens seemed almost destined to become a well-known sculptor. Born in Dublin in 1848, he came to the United States at age six months when his family left Ireland because of the potato famine. He grew up in New York City, spending much of his time after school in his father's shoemaking shop. When the boy was thirteen years old, his father asked him what trade he wanted to learn. Saint-Gaudens replied: "I should like it if I could do something which would help me be an artist."

His father consented. He had seen enough of his son's sketches on the walls of the shop and on fences to be convinced of his talent. He therefore arranged that Saint-Gaudens begin an apprenticeship with a Frenchman, a cutter of stone cameos. Saint-Gaudens worked with that man for a period of three and one-half years, recalling the experience later as one of "miserable slavery." He next worked three years for a shell-cameo carver, who allowed him to work an hour each day with clay. At this time he began to take drawing lessons at Cooper Union after work, and soon he was also studying at the National Academy of Design.

Saint-Gaudens' father watched his son's development closely, recognizing an exceptional artistic talent. When the son was nineteen, his father offered to send him to Paris, where he might better develop his talents. Saint-Gaudens arrived in Paris in 1867. After several months he was admitted to the Ecole des Beaux-Arts. There he studied for over two years, supporting himself by cutting cameos. In 1870, at the outbreak of the Franco-Prussian War, he left Paris and traveled to Rome.

In Rome Saint-Gaudens began to work seriously as a sculptor. He modeled Hiawatha, which eventually attracted the attention of a wealthy American, Montgomery Gibbs. Through Gibbs Saint-Gaudens was introduced to another American, who commissioned marble copies of the ancient busts of Demosthenes and Cicero. With these commissions completed, Saint-Gaudens was well on his way as a sculptor when he returned to New York in 1872. He remained in New York several months, then returned again to Rome where for a time he continued to model a variety of pieces, including portrait heads and copies from Greek and Roman antiquity.

The first piece to establish Saint-Gaudens' American reputation as a sculptor was a monument of Admiral David Farragut. Shortly after Farragut's death in 1870, the Farragut Monument Association was formed to choose a sculptor for an appropriate memorial figure. Saint-

163

Gaudens was considered, but the committee preferred the more established sculptor John Quincy Adams Ward. Ward, too busy, withdrew in favor of Saint-Gaudens, who was awarded the commission in December 1876.

Saint-Gaudens began to model the Farragut statue in early 1878, completing it in 1880. The model was cast in bronze in Paris and transported to New York City, where it was unveiled in May 1881. Critics immediately hailed the Farragut monument, as they later did the standing Lincoln. A rugged naturalism dominated the statue, yet fused with it was a heroic American spirit. A new era had begun in American sculpture.

Over the next twenty-seven years Saint-Gaudens produced several other well-known monument pieces, including the *Puritan* and the *Adams Memorial* — copies of which may be seen at the Saint-Gaudens National Historic Site in Cornish. In addition to these sculptures, he was also well known for his reliefs and cameos. During the last years of his life Saint-Gaudens spent most of his time at Cornish, where he continued to work as a sculptor until his death at age fifty-nine. He died on August 3, 1907.

AUGUSTA SAINT-GAUDENS

HER NAME was Augusta; his, Augustus. When they first met, they both confessed they hated their names. And then they laughed.

Their names were the same and, when they first met, their aspirations were similar. He was determined to be a sculptor; she wished to be a painter. These aspirations remained with them when they married, but soon afterward something changed. Only Augustus succeeded as an artist, becoming recognized as early as 1880. In that same year Augusta put away her paints and brushes and never painted again.

It is difficult to say whether Augusta Saint-Gaudens, neé Homer, would have developed into an outstanding painter, had she persisted. Her copies of paintings were excellent, and she received many compliments on them. Whether she possessed sufficient talent to be genuinely creative is, however, uncertain. Augusta was herself aware that copying and painting require different resources. When she was first taking painting lessons, she complained, "I am improving in my working from life but at the same time seem to be losing my power of copying for they are really so different."

Although the question of Augusta's artistic ability remains open, it can be said with some certainty that her failure to develop her potential as a painter was typical for most artistic women of the time. Perhaps the greatest obstacle she faced was the prevalent attitude that art was not a suitable career for women. Art was viewed as a proper "accomplishment" for a well brought-up young wom-

Augusta Saint-Gaudens. Courtesy Baker Library.

165

an. Mrs. Ellis' widely popular *Family Monitor and Domestic Guide* advised that painting or drawing "is, of all other occupations [for a young lady], the one most calculated to keep the mind from brooding upon self, and to maintain that general cheerfulness which is a part of social and domestic duty."

Augusta's upbringing reflected the period's social attitudes toward women and art. Born in 1848, she was raised in relative comfort in Roxbury, outside Boston. As a child she displayed early a talent for music, but problems with her hearing necessitated that she forego any serious musical study. Talented also in drawing and painting, she was encouraged in this at school. Her encouragement, however, was not the same as that which young Augustus received from his father. Her drawing abilities were not viewed as something for a possible career, but rather as a special refinement.

Other obstacles impeded a woman's development as an artist. Nude models, for example, were unavailable to women painters and sculptors. Since the beginning of art academies in the sixteenth and early seventeenth centuries, life drawing from nude, usually male, models was central to all serious training programs. Female models were employed by individuals and private academies, but female nudes were not allowed in most public art schools until 1850. But whether male or female nude models were used, women were forbidden to see them. As late as 1893, women students in London were not admitted to life drawing classes. When women were finally admitted, the models were partially draped.

When Augusta first came to Rome in 1873, life drawing classes were closed to women. Access to instruction in painting was also at times a problem, as many painters did not want to bother teaching "young ladies." Augusta spent considerable time in the galleries of Rome painting copies of masterpieces. She excelled

at it, and perhaps it somewhat suited her artistic temperament. But no doubt she partly pursued this course because it was the training most readily available to her.

Despite the difficulties, Augusta persisted. When she married in 1877 she still wanted to paint, but the desire slowly waned. Lack of time was the first obstacle that marriage brought. In addition to finding and organizing an apartment and studio in Paris, she managed the couple's financial matters, including those connected with Augustus' work. Whenever there were guests, Augusta attended to them, insuring that Augustus was not disturbed too often. After one evening she wrote her mother, "They all stayed till nearly twelve and my rooms were pretty full. . . . I wonder when I shall ever do any painting again."

She never found the time. In the latter part of 1878 Augusta painted three portraits, two of which she sold. She was greatly excited about these developments, but she could not sustain the effort. Unable to view her painting as primary or to consider it a full-time occupation, she subordinated her artistic interests to Augustus. In 1879 she began to help in a minor way with modeling details for the Farragut statue in clay. "I have been modeling some on the sword hilt and feel quite elated that I can do something of the kind," she wrote in a letter. One year later she gave up painting completely.

Augusta's decision to stop painting coincided with the birth of her first child on September 28, 1880. The rest of her long life was devoted largely to caring for their son Homer and to looking after Augustus' financial affairs. She appears to have been relatively happy, although at times she suffered depressions. After Augustus' death in 1907, she spent much of her time arranging exhibitions of her husband's works and establishing a permanent memorial for him at Cornish. In 1926, at age seventy-eight, Augusta died.

Rudyard Kipling in Brattleboro

THE CORNISH Colony in New Hampshire became the best-known domicile for artists in the Upper Valley. For writers, painters, poets, and wealthy patrons of the arts, including politicians, at the turn of the century, it was the fashionable place to be. During his presidency, Woodrow Wilson made Cornish his summer White House, residing three summers (1913-1915) at the home of the novelist Winston Churchill. But not all famous artists who came to the Upper Valley flocked to Cornish. One notable exception was Rudyard Kipling.

Born in Bombay in 1865, Kipling became before 1900 one of Great Britain's most popular writers. Noted in particular for his stories and poems based on life in India, his name still evokes an image of that country. Brattleboro, Vermont, is as different from India as can be imagined, and few associate this Upper Valley town with Kipling. They should. Kipling lived there four years, and his connection with the town played an influential part in his life.

Kipling first arrived in Brattleboro on February 17, 1892. "Thirty below freezing!" he later recalled. "It was inconceivable till one stepped into it at midnight, and the first shock of that clear, still air took away the breath as does a plunge into sea-water. A walrus sitting on a woolpack was our host in his sleigh, and he wrapped us in hairy goatskin coats, caps that came down over the ears, buffalo robes and blankets, and yet more buffalo-robes till we, too, looked like walruses and moved almost as gracefully." Having lived only in India and southern England, Kipling had never experienced such intense cold.

Kipling might never have known such a winter, had he not met and married Carrie Balestier. Carrie was from Brattleboro. But Kipling met her in London through her older brother Wolcott, himself a minor novelist, who had come to London at the end of 1888 to arrange for cheap American reprints of popular English books. Within a short time Wolcott was well established in London, where he was widely respected in various literary circles. Wolcott represented Kipling as his publishing agent. They met sometime in 1890, and their business

Wolcott Balestier, about 1890. Courtesy the Howard Rice Collection.

relationship quickly evolved into friendship. The two men began collaboration on a novel titled *The Naulahka, a Novel of East and West*. And Kipling met Carrie, who had traveled to England to help tend her brother's household.

Marriage was apparently not on Kipling's mind when he first met Carrie, and some biographers have even speculated that the two would not have married, had

167

it not been for the untimely death of Wolcott. On a trip to Germany in December 1891, Wolcott contracted typhoid fever and died within eight days. He was thirty years old. As he lay dying, he reportedly commended the care of his family to Kipling. True or not, Kipling did hurry back to London, where in mid-January 1892 he married Carrie. Shortly after their marriage, they boarded a ship and moved to Brattleboro.

Despite the unfamiliar cold, Kipling loved the Vermont and New Hampshire hills along the Connecticut River. By his second day in Brattleboro, he had ex-plored the area sufficiently to know that he wanted a house high on a hillside with a view of Mount Monadnock. His move to the Upper Valley brought no regrets. If he had not had later difficulties with his young brother-in-law, Kipling would probably have remained longer than four years.

By 1892 Kipling was already well known as a writer in Great Britain, but his fame in the United States lagged behind. In Brattleboro most residents considered Carrie's new husband to be a quiet, unassuming young man, who generally dressed in old country clothes.

"Naulakha." From The Vermonter, April 1899.

Kipling happily remained unrecognized in the town. He did not write much during his first year in Brattleboro, but tended to other matters. As soon as the winter snows melted, he and Carrie contracted to have their house built off Black Mountain Road. The house, which Kipling said lay on a long slope like a ship mounting an ocean swell, was named "Naulakha," in memory of the book Kipling and Wolcott had written together. At the end of the year the Kiplings' first child, a daughter named Josephine, was born in Brattleboro. A second daughter, Elsie, was born there in 1896.

Almost a year after the move to Brattleboro, Kipling experienced a renewed creative impulse, and between November 1892 and March 1895 he wrote the two volumes of *The Jungle Books.* Set in India but written in Vermont, these two books became the biggest sellers of all Kipling's works. Another work written largely in Brattleboro was *Captains Courageous,* the only one of Kipling's stories set in America, with all characters based on American types. Dr. James Conland, a Brattleboro physician who had been a sailor and became a lifelong friend of Kipling's, provided the author with many tales about sea life. To prepare for this book, Kipling also made three trips to Gloucester, Massachusetts, where within a short time he acquired an acquaintance with the area's fishing life. The tale has an authenticity greatly admired by American readers.

Kipling's increasing popularity led predictably to the loss of anonymity he had enjoyed when first in Brattleboro. By 1894 the Kiplings were hounded by summer sightseers hoping to catch a glimpse of the famous writer. Newspapermen also appeared in the town, searching for any hint of scandal. Because of intrusions, the Kiplings withdrew into stricter privacy, which in turn led to more gossip in the town about the distant and aloof Englishman.

The continued intrusions distressed Kipling, leading him to reconsider his decision to live in Brattleboro. Added to this distress was a confrontation in 1895 between Great Britain and the United States over a dispute about the frontier of Venezuela and British Guiana. Hoping to gain support in an election year, President Grover Cleveland made highly offensive remarks about England's policies in South America. For a time it appeared that Cleveland's remarks might result in war, and at the height of this crisis Kipling thought he might leave America.

Those disturbances influenced Kipling, but he finally decided to leave Brattleboro because of a continuing family dispute with Carrie's younger brother, Beatty Balestier. The family's youngest child, Beatty was spoiled and wild. He was known in Brattleboro as a good fellow who drank, was free with money whenever he had any, and who drove his horses at a gallop up and down the narrow Vermont roads. When Kipling first arrived in Brattleboro, his relationship with his brother-in-law seemed excellent. They were often together, and it was even arranged that Beatty should care for "Naulakha" whenever the Kiplings were away.

But Beatty's drunkenness and constant need of financial help quickly soured his relationship with Kipling.

Especially annoying to Kipling was the fact that the family disputes — usually arguments between Carrie and Beatty — became a primary topic of gossip in Brattleboro. The quarrel with Beatty over his drinking and financial difficulties worsened when Kipling's brother-in-law filed a petition for bankruptcy in March 1896. Believing stories started by Beatty, many in town blamed the Kiplings for Beatty's financial problems, because they refused to loan him money. The family feud widened in the following days. Town gossips noted that Carrie no longer consulted her Balestier relatives and that

Kipling had ceased paying visits to his in-laws. Scenting "copy" in the circulating rumors, newspaper reporters appeared in Brattleboro, where they were repulsed from "Naulakha" more brusquely than ever before.

Despite the increasing encroachments on his privacy, Kipling made an effort to continue writing and to sustain a normal routine apart from intrusions. That effort was completely shattered on May 6, 1892, when Beatty accosted Kipling on a country road and in a profusion of profanity accused Kipling of spreading lies about him in Brattleboro. After an

Beatty Balestier, early 1890s. Courtesy the Howard Rice Collection.

169

Maxfield Parrish

T HE CORNISH Colony, today little more than a memory, remains dominant in any talk about artists in the Upper Valley. Interestingly, only the colony itself is usually remembered, and not the artists. The fame accorded the individuals in their lifetimes passed with their deaths. Winston Churchill, one of America's best known novelists in the first years of the twentieth century, is today completely unknown. The poet Percy MacKaye is also largely forgotten, as are the sculptor Frances Grimes, the portrait painter William H. Hyde, the mural painters Kenyon and Louise Cox. Even Augustus Saint-Gaudens, the most prominent member of the Cornish Colony, is no longer accorded the widespread popularity he enjoyed in his lifetime.

The one exception is Maxfield Parrish, who in recent years has experienced a revival in the United States. Even in his lifetime, Parrish was an exception to the other artists residing in Cornish. He remained in the Upper Valley long after Cornish ceased to be fashionable and the other writers and painters had left. His art was also distinctly different from other works produced in Cornish.

Unlike Saint-Gaudens, Parrish did not produce singular and monumental works of art. He was essentially an illustrator of books, a designer of magazine covers and advertisements, a painter of reproduced color art prints. His subjects were not heroic, nor did he attempt to add a quality of idealism to a stark naturalistic pose. His drawings and paintings were playful and dreamy, and what he created was meant to be reproduced and sold as often as possible.

Parrish's work as an illustrator and designer represented in one sense the continuation of a long artistic tradition. Books had been illustrated in Egypt and China as early as the thirteenth or fourteenth century B.C. Artwork for magazines and advertisements was common, and in the nineteenth century color reproductions of European and American paintings became a lucrative business. Parrish's works were different, however. The singularity of a particular drawing or illustration was not important. The original intention of his art was its reproduction.

Parrish was not the only artist to produce works specifically intended for reproduction, but he was a forerunner in the field. Termed "commercial art," this reproduced art was often considered inferior to the more traditonal or "fine

Maxfield Parrish. Courtesy Virginia Colby.

arts.'' The introduction of a variety of reproduction techniques in the nineteenth century had made the development of commercial art possible. Wood engravings used to reproduce magazine illustrations were first replaced by steel engravings, which gave clearer and more distinct lines. In the 1890s the mechanical halftone process was developed, providing a rapid and accurate black-and-white reproduction. A few years later, techniques for color reproduction on a mass scale were introduced, and by the turn of the century numerous color illustrations began to appear in magazines.

These technical innovations led to a golden age for illustrators. Color photography was not yet perfected. All color illustration was done by artists like Parrish. Television did not exist, and the only mass media were the print media. The profusion of weekly and monthly magazines at the beginning of the nineteenth century were all illustrated, and Parrish was one of the best-known illustrators. His illustrations appeared on the covers of *Harper's Weekly*, *Scribner's*, *Collier's*, *Life*, and his pictures illustrated numerous books. He produced posters, advertisements, and color reproductions suitable for adorning empty walls, and he painted murals for a variety of architectural settings. Everywhere, it seemed, there was a Parrish. ''Parrish blue'' was a color, and the artist's name was a household word through the first half of the twentieth century.

While almost everything Parrish drew or painted became immediately known through countless reproductions, making him one of America's best known and popular artists, people really only knew his works. Parrish himself, as Coy Ludwig recounts in *Maxfield Parrish*, generally shunned the spotlight, choosing to live in the privacy and isolation of Plainfield, New Hampshire.

Born in Philadelphia on July 25, 1870, he was named Frederick Parrish. He later adopted his paternal grandmother's maiden name, Maxfield, as a middle name and subsequently used it professionally. His father owned a stationery store in Philadelphia, but he also painted regularly and often thought of becoming a full-time painter. He was determined his son should have every opportunity to develop his artistic talents, and when the boy was still young, he taught him the techniques of drawing and how to observe objects in nature. This training guided Parrish when he first began to think of a career. Entering Haverford College in 1888, he planned to become an architect. Four years later, after completion of his studies at Haverford, he enrolled at the Pennsylvania Academy of Fine Arts, fully committed to pursuing a career in art.

Parrish's career as an artist flourished almost immediately. In 1894, shortly before he concluded his studies at the Academy of Fine Arts, he received his first major commission. He was asked to paint an Old King Cole mural and other wall decorations for the Mask and Wig Club of the University of Pennsylvania in Philadelphia. When completed, the humorous painting received immediate attention from critics.

In 1895 Parrish spent the summer in Europe, visiting galleries and museums. Upon his return to the United States he established a studio in Philadelphia with his new bride, Lydia Austin, herself a painter. Parrish remained in Philadelphia, producing book and magazine illustrations and advertisement designs until 1898, when he decided to move to Plainfield, New Hampshire. The move was motivated in part by Parrish's parents. Several years earlier his father had quit his stationery business to become a full-time painter. Stephen Parrish was generally successful as an artist, and his paintings were regularly exhibited throughout the country. He was best known for his etchings, especially those depicting New England coastal scenes. Attracted by the colony of artists gathered along the Connecticut River, he had chosen to settle in Cornish.

Parrish followed his father to the area, purchasing a large tract of land a few hundred yards from the Cornish line in the township of Plainfield. Here he

designed and built a house called ''The Oaks.'' The move from Philadelphia required a bold decision. For a young artist, commissions were easier to obtain in a major city than in rural New Hampshire, but the move did not impede Parrish's career, nor did he ever regret his decision. Long after all the other writers and artists had left Cornish, Parrish remained in Plainfield, living there sixty-eight years until his death in 1966.

The privacy that Parrish found in Plainfield suited his temperament. He particularly enjoyed the winter months, when few visitors interrupted his routine. During much of his career he arose early, eating breakfast at 5:30 A.M. The early hours were the most creative for him, and he used them to design compositions, to draw, and to do other work requiring total concentration. When he first came to Plainfield, he also spent time working on and expanding his house. Originally a modest few rooms, ''The Oaks'' became one of the most outstanding residences in the area. It was so frequently the subject of

magazine articles that Parrish remarked: ''The place has been so photographed that the corners are getting rounded.''

In addition to designing and constructing his house, Parrish also made a variety of objects which adorned it. His studio contained a machine shop, where he made fine hinges, latches, and other utilitarian objects used at ''The Oaks.'' The machine shop also provided relaxation after a period of concentrated painting. In many respects Parrish was self-sufficient. His artistic talents extended beyond an ability to draw and paint pictures, and he was able to create and shape his environment as he wished. The isolation he sought in New Hampshire no doubt related to his desire to create his own world. There, generally alone and apart from others, he could devise and construct whatever he wished.

Parrish's fairytale figures and scenes seem to be a reflection and extension of the same private, semi-isolated life he led in Plainfield. For almost seventy years he drew and painted pictures, stopping only

174

'ASPET', CORNISH, N. H., June 20, 1905.

A MASQUE OF 'OURS'

THE GODS AND THE GOLDEN BOWL.

Being a Mumming Show Given in Celebration of the Twentieth Anniversary of the Founding of the Cornish Colony by Augustus and Augusta Saint-Gaudens.

Jupiter,	Mr. BLAIR,
Hermes,	Mr. MACKAYE,
Pluto,	Mr. COX,
Pan,	Mr. ADAMS,
Chronos,	Mr. PLATT,
Mars,	Mr. STILLMAN,
Chiron,	Mr. M. PARRISH,
Apollo,	Mr. FULLER,
And A Countryman,	
Charon,	Mr. HAPGOOD,
Orpheus,	Mr. WHITING,
Silenus,	Mr. HART,
Leander,	Mr. HYDE,
Nestor,	Mr. S. PARRISH,
Priam,	Mr. WALKER,
Phidias,	Mr. L. SAINT-GAUDENS.

Satyrs and Fauns by Messrs. Beaman, Herring, Thrasher, Hoppin, Fraser-Campbell, Walker, Rublee and Elliot.

Juno,	Mrs. MacKAYE,	Cupid,	Miss WARD,
Neptune,	Miss F. J. SLADE,	Hero,	Mrs. HYDE,
Diana,	Mrs. CHURCHILL,	Clotho,	Mrs. L. SAINT-GAUDENS,
Iris, as Prologue,	Miss GRIMES,	Lachesis,	Mrs. WOOD,
Venus,	Miss PARRISH,	Atropos,	Mrs. WALKER,
Minerva,	Mrs. SHIPMAN,	Clio,	Miss C. ARNOLD,
Proserpina,	Mrs. FULLER,	Melpomene,	Miss M. NICHOLS,
Ceres,	Mrs. HOUSTON,	Terpsichore,	Mrs. RUBLEE.
Eurydice,	Mrs. WHITING,	Thalia,	Miss ISHAM,
Thetis,	Mrs. COX,	Euterpe,	Mrs. PARRISH,
Calypso,	Miss G. LAWRENCE,	Erato,	Mrs. MANN,
Europa,	Miss G. ARNOLD,	Urania,	Miss E. SLADE,
Pomona,	Mrs. ELLIOT,	Polyhymnia,	Miss R. NICHOLS,
Flora,	Miss F. ARNOLD,	Calliope,	Mrs. TAYLOR,
Circe,		Fame,	Miss KENNEDY.

Dryads, Bacchantes, Nymphs, etc., by Mrs. Shurtleff, Miss MacKaye, Miss Margaret Beaman, Miss E. Devigne, Miss E. M. Devigne, Miss T. Devigne, Miss Stewart, Miss Bohm, Miss Stuart, Miss S. Smoot, Miss Smoot, Miss M. Smoot, Miss Hardy, Miss C. Fuller, Miss E. Shipman, Miss C. Cox, Miss S. Hyde, Miss S. Platt, Miss M. Churchill, and Masters C. Fuller, R. Mann, A. Cox, L. Cox, W. Platt, R. Platt and R. MacKaye.

Atalanta,   Psyche,

The Prologue by Mr. MacKaye.   The Masque by Mr. Shipman.

The Stage under the direction of Mr. Blair.

The Music by Mr. Whiting.

CHURCH AT NORWICH, VERMONT. *Also known as* PEACEFUL NIGHT.
Oil on panel, 1950. © B&B, USA, 1951. Art from the archives of Brown & Bigelow.

in 1962, when at age ninety-one his health began to deteriorate. Most striking about the art he produced during those many years is its general lack of variation in theme or style. Usually he chose a fairy tale or an adventure story, such as *The Arabian Nights*, as a theme, or he depicted dream images of long-ago times and make-believe worlds . Even his later paintings of New England scenes and landscapes, such as *Church at Norwich, Vermont* or *Afterglow*, appear more dreamlike than real. And almost every picture is awash in romantic colors.

The sameness of these images is even more striking when you consider they were produced during years of violent conflicts. Parrish's productive years span two world wars, the Depression, and years of labor and racial strife, yet images of a violent reality rarely intrude into his pictures. Again and again he reproduced a romanticized world. Perhaps it can be concluded that Parrish's art was simply another part of the reclusive life he created for himself in Plainfield. There, in a world separated from the social and political events of his times, he depicted an equally isolated aesthetic world. The question still remains why these private images had and still have such widespread public appeal in the United States.

From Huggins Folly to Aspet: A Final Glance at the Upper Valley's History

PERCHED ABOVE the Connecticut River in an open field, Saint-Gaudens' house is visible from afar. Its neatly mowed lawn, sloping down toward the river, appears as a singular interruption among the trees, and the white brick house with its large porch is distinctive even at a distance. Today the house is a National Historic Site, administered since 1965 by the National Park Service, in cooperation with the trustees of the Saint-Gaudens Memorial established by Augusta Saint-Gaudens. A part of the Upper Valley's history has been preserved.

Other memorials to the past can be found in the Upper Valley, though many lie in states of decay or abandonment, rather than tended preservation. A stroll almost anywhere in the woods reveals tumbled-down stone walls passing among trees, up steep inclines, around immovable boulders. It seems scarcely possible that this land was ever cleared, that settlers toiled here to plant and harvest crops. The stone walls and perhaps a few abandoned cellar holes are the only remaining testimony of the hardships encountered during the early years of settlement. Here and there small cemeteries can also be found, far from any present-day communities, and everywhere are abandoned and overgrown roads, leading, it seems, nowhere. On numerous rivers and streams are the broken remains of former dams, and in many towns stand abandoned factories and mills. All are reminders of the past, of the transformations from farming to in-

"Huggins Folly" and barn, before 1885. This was probably the way the house appeared when Saint-Gaudens first arrived in Cornish in April 1885. Courtesy Saint-Gaudens National Historic Site.

dustry, of populations shifting away from isolated farms, of changes leading to the twentieth century.

Preserved and abandoned sites are the most visible markers of Upper Valley history, but others abound in less open places. Most frequently the hidden signs are simply obscured by the contemporary use we make of things. A converted building does not necessarily remind us of its past. But almost anywhere you poke your nose there are clues to the past, and invariably the clues reveal patterns in the region's historical development. Saint-Gaudens' house in Cornish is a perfect example. Because it is a monument to a specific period in Cornish history, we often overlook the fact that the house experienced numerous changes in the course of the Upper Valley's settlement and subsequent development.

Saint-Gaudens did not build his house in Cornish, though he made considerable changes and improvements. When he first rented the house in 1885, it had stood for a considerable part of the town's life. In fact, the early years of local

settlement are the only period absent in the house's long existence. Even without knowing the exact year, construction can be dated at sometime in the opening years of 1800. Built of brick, the house most assuredly was not a crude farm house, as were the first shelters in the Upper Valley. It was also something grander than the usual frame houses built when life improved in the first decades after settlement. Its size, even discounting the later additions made by Saint-Gaudens, sets it apart from other houses. Such a large house was obviously erected during a moment in Cornish history when a certain wealth had been achieved and future growth was expected.

The house was probably built in 1805, though this is not certain. That period was a fast-paced time for Cornish and the Upper Valley. Farming was profitable in the area, and most towns were growing rapidly. Cornish, for example, nearly doubled its population between 1790 and 1810, growing from 982 residents to 1,606. Economic prosperity and rapid growth inspired various enterprises to improve or to develop markets in the Upper Valley. The greatest undertaking was the attempt to improve transportation to the area. To facilitate river traffic, locks and canals were built at the different waterfalls on the Connecticut. To compete with the river trade, numerous turnpikes to and through the Upper Valley were proposed.

The excitement generated by the thought of large, and perhaps fast profits to be made from road construction swept through the entire state of New Hampshire. In the early 1800s the "turnpike craze" infected a large portion of the populace, and by 1810 close to fifty turnpike companies had been incorporated. Most never completed a road. In Cornish two brothers, Samuel and Jonas Huggins, caught the "bug," and together they devised a scheme to profit from a proposed cross-state turnpike through Newport, Cornish Flat, and Meriden. Anticipating considerable traffic along this road, the brothers built a large brick house to serve as an inn or tavern, as it was then called. Judging by the house's size, the two hoped to attract many travelers.

In that period of unlimited enthusiasm about the Upper Valley's future, Jonas and Samuel Huggins no doubt thought of an inn as a risk-free investment. Without waiting for the turnpike to be constructed, they built their house and waited. The anticipated traffic never arrived. A turnpike through Cornish went south from the covered bridge, and nothing was built where the Huggins were located. Eventually the large brick structure became known as "Huggins Folly."

Despite the changed circumstances the Huggins were able to hold onto their house for twenty years. In 1824, however, they sold it and left Cornish. Both followed the general westward migration, one brother moving to Illinois, the other apparently to Canada. Their moves typified what was happening in Cornish and other Upper Valley towns. Great expectations had seemed justified at the beginning of the nineteenth century, when the brothers built their house, but twenty years later those expectations proved for many to be ephemeral dreams. Between the years 1820 and 1830 Cornish's population declined from 1,701 to 1,687, and with one exception between 1830 and 1840, it continued to decline through the rest of the nineteenth century. By 1890 only 934 residents remained in the town, fewer than in 1790.

Austin Tyler and John Gove purchased the house from the Huggins, and, according to Hugh Wade in *A Brief History of Cornish*, it degenerated "into a house of ill fame." Whether or not that is true is difficult to say. Local histories of the nineteenth century do not elaborate on the taboo subject of prostitution, and no records tell of the house's use as a bordello. Known for certain is the fact that under Tyler and Gove's ownership, the open land around "Huggins Folly" was used as a stopping station for sheep being transported to market.

The house's connection with sheep reflected wider patterns of development in Cornish. Sheep became vital to the town; many were raised there and even more passed through on their way to market. The Cornish-Windsor bridge was a major crossing point over the Connecticut River, and for several years sheep were its major users. In 1825 over 9,000 sheep crossed the bridge. The number increased steadily in the following years, reaching a peak in 1838 when 14,084 sheep passed over the bridge.

The many sheep entering Cornish did not always pass through immediately. The town served as a waystation for sheep, and farmers either rested there before proceeding to Boston, or waited until arrangements could be made to transport their sheep and other goods down the river by barge. While stopped in Cornish the sheep needed to graze, and the land around "Huggins Folly" provided good forage. Tyler and Gove owned the house from 1824 to 1839, the same years that sheep farming was at its height in the Upper Valley, and it can be assumed sheep grazed there most of those years. When sheep farming began its decline, fewer and fewer sheep passed into Cornish, and the meadow at "Huggins Folly" ceased to be used for grazing.

Small mills were built in most towns throughout the Upper Valley, including Cornish. Among the mills established there was a fulling mill on the Blow-Me-Down Brook, just below "Huggins Folly." The year the fulling mill opened is not known, but in 1839 Walter and John Mercer purchased "Huggins Folly" to use as living quarters for the workers in their fulling mill on the brook below. A fulling mill might have been in operation on the Blow-Me-Down Brook at an earlier date, and if so, Tyler and Gove probably also used the house for workers. Whatever the date, the use made of the large, brick house reflected the wider pattern of change in the Upper Valley from agriculture to manufacturing.

Fulling mills in the mid-nineteenth century performed a separate function in the manufacture of cloth. In these mills, cloth was cleansed and thickened by a process of washing and pressing between rollers. Unfortunately, workers in the early Upper Valley mills left few written documents, and nothing is known of actual working conditions in the Blow-Me-Down mill or of life at "Huggins Folly." Use of the house for workers was relatively short, however. As technology became more advanced, the fulling process was integrated into the operations of larger mills, eliminating the need for fulling mills.

The disappearance of fulling and other smaller mills marked the end of manufacturing in Cornish. Waterpower in the town was not sufficient to support larger factories. The newer, larger mills became concentrated along major waterfalls in towns such as Lebanon and Claremont, while smaller ones like Mercer's were simply abandoned and never replaced. The workers vanished with the mills, and for several years "Huggins Folly" stood empty, again a symbol of changing fortunes in the Upper Valley.

In 1884 "Huggins Folly" changed ownership twice. The house was first deeded to William Mercer, son of Walter Mercer, and then sold to Charles C. Beaman. Beaman was a lawyer in New York City, who in the latter part of the nineteenth century began purchasing land in Cornish. By 1894 Beaman owned a thousand acres in the town, including most of the land along the Connecticut River from the Windsor Bridge to Plainfield. Beaman himself built a summer home in Cornish in 1884, and he was the man who persuaded Saint-Gaudens to spend the summer of 1885 in the town.

Beaman rented the house to Saint-Gaudens for six years, selling it to him finally in 1891 for twenty-five hundred dollars plus a bas-relief of himself. Saint-Gaudens and his wife Augusta renamed "Huggins Folly," calling it "Aspet," after his father's birthplace in France. The name and the use of the brick house as an artist's residence was something new, but once again it reflected a pattern in the Upper Valley's development.

Throughout the years different uses made of this one house mirrored broader patterns in the area's economic history. Built in an era of growth, the house was meant to serve as an inn along an expanding network of transportation. When that failed, it hosted sheep during the years dominated by sheep farming. It housed workers when small mills became a growing part of the area's economy. It stood empty when Cornish and many other small towns experienced continuing decline. When Saint-Gaudens arrived to spend the summer, it witnessed the advent of summer tourism. The reflection of these broader patterns continues even today. Tourism has achieved a permanent niche in the economy of the Upper Valley, and the conversion of "Aspet" into a National Historic Site insures that the house will be a tourist attraction indefinitely.

The house is a memorial, but it preserves more than the memory of Saint-Gaudens and the Cornish Colony. Its history contains much of the history of Cornish and the Upper Valley. Similar memorials are present in stone walls, in old houses, in converted buildings, almost everywhere, if only we look closely.

"Aspet," about 1900. View looking south. Courtesy Saint-Gaudens National Historic Site.

SUGGESTIONS FOR FURTHER READING

Whenever I am asked to recommend a book on the history of the Upper Valley, I always hesitate before answering. A general history of the Upper Valley does not exist; information must be sought from a variety of sources. For example, Harold F. Wilson's *The Hill Country of Northern New England* provides considerable detail on the agricultural and economic development of the area; Edwin M. Bacon's *The Connecticut River and the Valley of the Connecticut* remains one of the best books on the settlement and growth of the entire valley; William A. Haviland and Marjory W. Power's *The Original Vermonters* is an invaluable resource book for the history of the Indians who first occupied the land. Other books cover different events and developments, but references to the Upper Valley are usually to be found only within larger histories of Vermont or New Hampshire or New England.

Knowing particular events or persons makes it easier to recommend further readings. Specific works can be connected to specific topics. The following list is intended to make such connections. For every chapter a few works have been chosen from those I have used in my research.

1 BEFORE EUROPEAN DISCOVERY

Day, Gordon. "The Identity of the Sokokis." *Ethnohistory*, Summer 1965, pp. 237-249.

Day, Gordon. "Western Abenaki." In *Handbook of North American Indians*, edited by Bruce G. Trigger, vol. 15, pp. 148-159. Washington D.C.: Smithsonian Institute, 1978.

Haviland, William A., and Power, Marjory W. *The Original Vermonters*. Hanover and London: University Press of New England, 1981.

Snow, Dean R. *The Archaeology of New England*. New York and London: Academic Press, 1980.

2 MAJOR ROBERT ROGERS' RAID ON THE ST. FRANCIS INDIANS

Cuneo, John R. *Robert Rogers of the Rangers*. New York: Oxford University Press, 1959.

Day, Gordon. "Rogers' Raid In Indian Tradition." *Historical New Hampshire*, June 1962, pp. 3-17.

Peckham, Howard H. *The Colonial Wars, 1689-1762*. Chicago and London: University of Chicago Press, 1964.

Rogers, Robert. *Journals*. Reprinted from the original edition of 1765, with an introduction by Howard H. Peckham. New York: Corinth Books, 1961.

3 THE AGE OF SELF-SUFFICIENT FARMING

Belknap, Jeremy. *The History of New Hampshire*. 3 vols. Boston: 1791-1792.

Bidwell, Percy W., and Falconer, John I. *The History of Agriculture in the Northern United States, 1620-1860*. Washington D. C.: The Carnegie Institute of Washington, 1925.

Stilwell, Lewis D. *Migration from Vermont, 1776-1860*. Montpelier: Vermont Historical Society, 1948.

Williams, Samuel. *The Natural and Civil History of Vermont*. Walpole, N.H.: 1794.

Wilson, Harold F. *The Hill Country of Northern New England, Its Social and Economic History, 1790-1930*. New York: Columbia University Press, 1936.

4 THE FOUNDING OF DARTMOUTH COLLEGE

Blodgett, Harold W. *Samson Occom*. Hanover, N.H.: Dartmouth College Publications, 1935.

Chase, Frederick. *A History of Dartmouth College and the Town of Hanover, N.H.* Edited by John K. Lord. Concord, N.H.: The Rumford Press, 1913.

Love, William DeLoss. *Samson Occom, and the Christian Indians of New England*. Boston and Chicago: The Pilgrim Press, 1899.

McCallum, James D. *Eleazar Wheelock, Founder of Dartmouth College*. Hanover, N.H.: Dartmouth College Publications, 1939.

5 REBELLION IN THE UPPER VALLEY

Daniell, Jere R. *Experiment in Republicanism, New Hampshire Politics and the American Revolution, 1741-1794*. Cambridge: Harvard University Press, 1970.

Daniell, Jere R. "The Western Rebellion." *New Hampshire Profiles*, March 1976, pp. 26-28.

Rice, John L. "Dartmouth College and the State of New Connecticut, 1776-1782." *Papers and Proceedings of the Connecticut Valley Historical Society,* 1 (1876-1881), pp. 152-206.

6   THE CONNECTICUT RIVER

Bacon, Edwin M. *The Connecticut River and the Valley of the Connecticut.* New York and London: G. P. Putnam's & Sons, 1907.

Hayes, Lyman S. "The Navigation of the Connecticut River." *Proceedings of the Vermont Historical Society, 1916-1917,* (1918), pp. 49-86.

Jacobus, Melancthon W. *The Connecticut River Steamboat Story.* Hartford, Conn.: The Connecticut Historical Society, 1956.

Upham, George B. "Early Navigation on the Connecticut." *The Granite Monthly,* July 1919, pp. 301-305.

Whittlesey, Charles W. *Crossing and Recrossing the Connecticut River.* New Haven: The Tuttle, Morehouse & Taylor Co., 1938.

7   LOGGING ON THE CONNECTICUT

Pike, Robert. *Tall Trees, Tough Men.* New York and London: W. W. Norton & Co., 1967.

Waterman, William R. *Mills Olcott, 1774-1845.* Hanover, N.H.: Dartmouth College, 1969.

8   NEW HAMPSHIRE TURNPIKES IN THE UPPER VALLEY

Goldthwait, J. W. "Six Old New Hampshire Highways." *New Hampshire Highways,* July 1932, pp. 1-7; August 1932, pp. 12-19.

Upham, George B. "The Great Road to the North, Through the Upper Connecticut Valley." *The Granite Monthly,* February 1920, pp. 50-56.

Waterman, William R. "The Fourth New Hampshire Turnpike." *Historical New Hampshire,* November 1960, pp. 1-25.

Wood, Frederic J. *The Turnpikes of New England, and Evolution of the Same Through England, Virginia, and Maryland.* Boston: Marshall Jones, 1919.

9   THE ORFORD RIDGE HOUSES

Hodgson, Alice Doan. *Thanks to the Past, The Story of Orford, N.H.* Orford, N.H.: Historical Facts Publications, 1965.

Hodgson, Alice Doan. *Samuel Morey, Inventor Extraordinary of Orford, N.H.* Orford, N.H.: Historical Facts Publications, 1961.

10   NATHAN SMITH, FOUNDER OF THE DARTMOUTH MEDICAL SCHOOL

Chapman, Carleton B. *Dartmouth Medical School, The First 175 Years.* Hanover, N.H.: University Press of New England, 1973.

Donaldson, Gordon A. "The Legacy of Nathan Smith." *Harvard Medical Alumni Bulletin,* February 1981, pp. 20-28.

Smith, Emily. *The Life and Letters of Nathan Smith, M.B., M.D.* New Haven: Yale University Press, 1914.

11   DARTMOUTH AND THE DARTMOUTH COLLEGE CASE

Bartlett, Irving H. *Daniel Webster.* New York: W. W. Norton & Co., 1978.

Morin, Richard W. "Will to Resist, The Dartmouth College Case." *Dartmouth Alumni Magazine,* April 1969.

Shirley, John M. *The Dartmouth College Causes and the Supreme Court of the United States.* St. Louis: G. I. Jones & Co., 1879.

12   MARY MARSHALL DYER AND THE ENFIELD SHAKERS

Andrews, Edward D. *The People Called Shakers.* New York: Oxford University Press, 1953.

Brodie, Fawn. *No Man Knows My History, The Life of Joseph Smith, The Mormon Prophet.* New York: A. A. Knopf, 1957.

Faber, Doris. *The Perfect Life, The Shakers in America.* New York: Farrar, Straus & Giroux, 1974.

Robertson, Constance Noyes, ed. *Oneida Community, An Autobiography, 1851-1876.* Syracuse: Syracuse University Press, 1970.

13   THE NOYES ACADEMY IN CANAAN

Wallace, William Allen. *The History of Canaan, New Hampshire.* Concord, N.H.: The Rumford Press, 1910.

Siebert, Wilbur H. *Vermont's Anti-Slavery and Underground Railroad Record.* Columbus, Ohio: The Spahr & Glen Co., 1937.

14   THE TRANSFORMATION OF FARMING: FROM SELF-SUFFICIENCY TO SHEEP

Cutts, Mary P. S. *The Life and Times of William Jarvis.* New York: 1869.

Goldthwait, James Walter. "A Town that has gone Downhill." *The Geographical Review,* October 1927, pp. 527-552.

Wilson, Harold F. *The Hill Country of Northern New England* (see chapter 3).

15   THE NORTHERN RAILROAD

Frye, Harry A. "The Northern Railroad, A Brief History of the Northern R.R. of N.H." *The New England States Limited,* March 1982, pp. 6-17.

Harlow, Alvin F. *Steelways of New England.* New York: Creative Age Press, 1946.

Mead, Edgar. *Over the Hills to Woodstock, The Saga of the Woodstock RR.* Brattleboro, Vt.: The Stephen Greene Press, 1967.

Squires, James Duane. *Headlights and Highlights — The Northern Railroad of New Hampshire, 1844-1848.* New York: The Newcomen Society of England, American Branch, 1948.

16   EARLY MILLS OF LEBANON

Downs, Charles A. *History of Lebanon, N.H., 1761-1887.* Concord, N.H.: The Rumford Press, 1908.

Millen, Ethel R. *Historical Sketches of Early Lebanon.* Canaan, N.H.: Reporter Press, 1965.

17   THE DEWEY WOOLEN MILLS

A. G. Dewey Company 1836-1936. Brattleboro, Vt.: Vermont Printing Co., 1936.

Dublin, Thomas, ed. *Farm to Factory, Women's Letters, 1830-1860.* New York: Columbia University Press, 1981.

18   WINDSOR AND THE MACHINE TOOL INDUSTRY

Battison, Edwin A. *Muskets to Mass Production, The Men & the Times that Shaped American Manufacturing.* Windsor, Vt.: The American Precision Museum, 1976.
Broehl, Wayne. *Precision Valley, The Machine Tool Companies of Springfield, Vermont.* Englewood, N.J.: Prentice-Hall, 1959.

Rolt, L. T. C. *A Short History of Machine Tools.* Cambridge: MIT Press, 1965.

19   JUSTIN SMITH MORRILL AND THE LAND GRANT COLLEGES

Chandler, Elizabeth. "The Morrill Mausoleum." *The Interstate Journal,* September 1900.

Parker, William B. *Justin Smith Morrill.* Boston and New York: Houghton Mifflin Co., 1924.

20   THE TILDEN FEMALE SEMINARY

Woody, Thomas. *A History of Women's Education in the United States.* 2 vols. New York and Lancaster, Pa.: The Science Press, 1929.

Documents pertaining to the history of the Tilden Female Seminary can be found at the Lebanon Historical Society.

21   THE RISE OF THE DAIRY INDUSTRY

McFall, Robert J. *The New England Dairy Market.* Washington D. C.: 1925.

Wilson, Harold F. *The Hill Country of Northern New England* (see chapter 3).

22 SANATOGA SPRINGS

Crook, James K. *Mineral Waters of the United States and Their Therapeutic Uses.* New York and Philadelphia: Lea Bros. & Co., 1899.

Lee, W. Storrs. *The Green Mountains of Vermont.* New York: Henry Holt & Co., 1955.

Pike, Robert E. *Drama on the Connecticut.* Eatontown, N.J.: H-H Press, 1975.

23 MARY HITCHCOCK MEMORIAL HOSPITAL

Grow, Eugene J. "The Mary Hitchcock Hospital." *The Granite Monthly*, November 1896, pp. 247-258.

Land, Loretta C. *Hiram Hitchcock's Legacy, The History of the Mary Hitchcock Memorial Hospital School of Nursing.* Canaan, N.H.: Phoenix Publishing, 1980.

Richardson, Leon B. *Fifty Years of Service, A History of the Mary Hitchcock Memortial Hospital.* Hanover, N.H.: 1943.

24 SAINT-GAUDENS COMES TO CORNISH

Greer, Germaine. *The Obstacle Race, The Fortunes of Women Painters and Their Work.* New York: Farrar, Straus & Giroux, 1979.

Hess, Thomas B., and Baker, Elizabeth C., eds. *Art and Sexual Politics, Women's Liberation, Women Artists, and Art History.* New York: Macmillan, 1973.

Saint-Gaudens, Augustus. *The Reminiscences of Augustus Saint-Gaudens.* Edited and amplified by Homer Saint-Gaudens. New York: The Century Co., 1913.

Tharp, Louise H. *Saint-Gaudens and the Gilded Era.* Boston: Little, Brown, 1969.

25 RUDYARD KIPLING IN BRATTLEBORO

Amis, Kingsley. *Rudyard Kipling and his World.* New York: Scribner's, 1975.

Rice, Howard C. *Rudyard Kipling in New England.* Brattleboro, Vt.: Stephen Daye Press, 1936.

Van de Water, Frederic F. *Rudyard Kipling's Vermont Feud.* Weston, Vt.: The Countryman Press, 1937.

26 MAXFIELD PARRISH

Bland, David. *A History of Book Illustration.* Berkeley: University of California Press, 1969.

Ludwig, Coy. *Maxfield Parrish.* New York: Watson-Guptill, 1973.

Harthan, John P. *The History of the Illustrated Book, The Western Tradition.* London: Thomas & Hudson, 1981.

INDEX

Designed by Frank Lieberman

Typeset in Trump Medieval by
Whitman Press, Inc.

Printed on Warren Patina Matte by
The Murray Printing Company